Ruud Gullit

Ruud Gullit

PORTRAIT OF A GENIUS

HARRY HARRIS

AND

MARCEL VAN DER KRAAN

CollinsWillow

An Imprint of HarperCollins*Publishers*

First published in 1996
by CollinsWillow
an imprint of HarperCollins*Publishers*
London

© Harry Harris 1996

3 5 7 9 8 6 4

A CIP catalogue record for this book is
available from the British Library

ISBN 0 00 218756 6

Printed in Great Britain by
Caledonian International Book Manufacturing Ltd, Glasgow

Contents

To Linda ... a true Chelsea fan

Acknowledgements

My thanks to close Dutch friend and colleague Marcel van der Kraan for his expert views on the young Ruud Gullit; Godric Smith at the Prime Minister's No 10 Press Office; and of course to John Major himself for offering his views on Ruud. Plus all the other MPs, celebrities and people in the game who contributed their opinions. My thanks also go to Chelsea chairman Ken Bates, chief executive Colin Hutchinson, Ruud's UK advisors Jon and Phil Smith of First Artists Corporation, and Sky TV press officer Chris Haynes. The *Daily Mirror* provided a number of pictures for the book, and it was nice to get so much co-operation from my 'Fleet Street' colleagues, notably Michael Hart and photographer Frank Tewkesbury for the snap of Ruud winning the *Evening Standard* Footballer of the Month award for January, for which Ruud insisted all his team-mates appear! At publishers HarperCollins, praise too for Editorial Director Michael Doggart for recognising straight away my conviction that a biography of Ruud Gullit would make such fascinating reading; Tom Whiting for his patience and helpful suggestions; and Andrew Clark for his diligent sub-editing.

Finally, a special thanks to Dutch photographer Peter Smoulders for his excellent portfolio of Ruud Gullit pictures.

Introduction

Ruud Gullit is one of football's all-time greats. He has a reputation that puts him alongside Pele, Maradona, Cruyff, Charlton and Best in the world's elite. Indeed, some would say he is one of the most charismatic characters of them all. Gullit speaks five languages – Dutch, English, Italian, German and French. He sings and/plays bass guitar in a reggae band called Revelation Time and reached the Dutch Top Ten record charts with the single 'Not The Dancing Kind'. He has earned an average of £2 million for the last six years, wears £1,500 designer suits and has his own jet. A Bob Marley fan, Ruud Gullit dedicated his 1987 World Footballer of the Year award to Nelson Mandela.

His full roll of honour makes impressive reading: World Footballer of the Year (1987); European Footballer of the Year (1987); European Championships winner (1988); European Cup winner (1989, 1990); Italian League title (1988, 1992, 1993) and Dutch League title winner (1984, 1986, 1987); capped 66 times for Holland; scorer of 16 international goals. His transfer to AC Milan in 1987 cost what was then a world record £5.5 million.

The half-Dutch, half-Surinese superstar has few equals on the world soccer stage. At six foot one, this powerfully built athlete, with the trademark dreadlocks, has retained his immaculate physique even in his thirties. And he has brought far more than his reputation to English football. He has brought his charisma, style and sincerity, and his vast knowledge and experience – a potent combination fuelling his desire to transform Chelsea into a great club again. Gullit's mesmeric opening season in English football earned him endless accolades from the experts, but it was the fans who gave him his biggest honour at the climax of an exceptional year.

Second to Eric Cantona in the prestigious Football Writers' Association 'Footballer of the Year' vote, it was left to the fans of IPC Magazines to bestow on the multi-talented Dutchman the title of the Best International Performer of 1996.

A glittering array of celebrities gathered at the alternative 'Footie' awards night at Planet Hollywood on 6 May 1996 as Ruud was named the best international player in the UK. Readers of soccer magazines like the respected *World Soccer*, *Goal*, *90 Minutes*, *Soccer Stars* and *Shoot* voted Gullit the No 1, ahead of a stunning list of outstanding foreign stars attracted to English shores – Cantona, Georgi Kinkladze, David Ginola, Philippe Albert, Peter Schmeichel and Tony Yeboah.

Ruud had been neck and neck with Cantona for the major individual award of Footballer of the Year. Eventually, the Dutchman fell just 20 votes short of Cantona's total to finish second, with Liverpool's Robbie Fowler third. Cantona became only the fourth foreign player to win after Bert Trautman in 1956, Frans Thijssen in 1981, and Klinsmann in 1995.

Gullit has a weekly column in the *Sunday Express*. In his first, he said he had no problems about coming second to Cantona: 'If I had to assess my own performance, I would say I played pretty well this season and it was pleasing to be in the running for the Footballer of the Year award. I have no complaints about being beaten to the trophy by Eric Cantona either, because he has had such a tremendous season. This was a man who made a terrible mistake and paid for it, but he has been rewarded for what he has produced on the pitch ever since his return and I think that it is a great gesture by the English.'

On the day the Footballer of the Year was announced, Saturday 20 April, David Pleat nominated his Premiership Select XI with Cantona on the subs bench! The Sheffield Wednesday manager explained: 'Eric may be odds-on for the Football Writers' crown after almost single-handedly overhauling Newcastle's massive lead at the top of the table. But when it comes to Pleaty's All-Stars, I'm afraid he's on the bench. I must point out that it's no slur against France's finest export since vintage champagne. More a measure of my admiration for the fellow I've chosen ahead of him, the remarkable Ruud Gullit. The Dutch maestro looked the part as sweeper when he joined Chelsea but has been even more impressive since returning from injury and moving further forward. And, if I had any lingering doubts about picking him in preference to Cantona, it was banished by his performance against my Sheffield Wednesday side at Hillsborough. He looked nearer 23 than 33, the way he ran the show, and his passing and vision were second to none. He's on a different plain to most ordinary players. A brilliant long passer who coordinates his thinking and footwork as if by computer.'

That is the sort of esteem to which Ruud is held within the profession. Pleat's opinion is shared by Kevin Keegan. The Newcastle boss had splashed out £13 million on overseas signings, including Faustino Asprilla, Philippe Albert and David Ginola. Yet, Keegan revealed he had been interested in signing both Bergkamp and Gullit. 'We didn't get to the serious stage of signing Bergkamp, but I was interested in the summer before he joined Arsenal.

'Gullit was the one I was really interested in. Chelsea have been very clever and I was right when I thought he might prove to be the most exciting addition of the lot. I don't think we've ever had the depth of quality coming into the game from abroad that we have now. Club chairmen should be congratulated for putting money back into the game from television and sponsorship. Now it's up to our players to rise to the challenge and then we really will have a league to be proud of.'

Keegan enthused about the need of the Premiership to parade stars of the quality and drawing power of Eric Cantona, Dennis Bergkamp, Ruud Gullit, David Ginola and Georgi Kinkladze: 'They have given terrific value for money. We have been too insular in this country for too long. We may have given the game to the world but now the world has moved on. Some people want to protect our kids but bringing in these players from abroad will make the English game better, not worse. I say let the kids come through and challenge them for a place in the side. That will improve English football more than anything.'

Ruud made such an impact that the 1995/96 season drew to a close with speculation that he should coach the England team for the forthcoming World Cup campaign. A great compliment for Ruud, but Chelsea chairman Ken Bates was quick to dismiss claims that Ruud would link up with Glenn Hoddle as the new coaching partnership in succession to Terry Venables. Bates ruled out Gullit's involvement with the FA on any basis, full-time or part-time. He said: 'Gullit is under contract. There are no circumstances whatsoever under which Chelsea Football Club would be prepared to release him to go to the FA, and let me point out that he is on a full-time contract at Chelsea. If he has spare time to be considered for coaching sessions with the FA, then he would have time to be coaching Chelsea players!'

Ruud was flattered that he had been considered for a job with England: 'It is a great honour that someone would even think of it...but the most important thing for me right now that is that I want to continue playing. I never want to reflect on my career one day and think that I hung up my boots too soon. England might not be a practical proposition.

'The great English strength is that they play with heart but that is not enough when they step out of the Premiership. Sometimes it is better to use your mind. I prefer to give 90 per cent sometimes and save 10 per cent with a little intelligence.'

His impact within the Chelsea dressing room has been immense. Scottish international John Spencer's fascinating interview in the May 1996 edition of *Loaded* gave an insight into Gullit's motivating qualities. 'He turned up a week after everyone else for pre-season training. He walked in, smiled and came over and we were all like (open mouthed, gawp-like and stares), "It's the Master." He said, "Hi, I'm Ruud" and I said, "I know who you are … er … I'm John Spencer." It was weird seeing him there.'

After the initial shock, and Ruud's early reluctance to risk being seen as the 'Big I am', it was an education being in his presence. Spencer added: 'He never goes around trying to be better than anyone else, he gets stick off me and Wisey like anyone else and he gives it back too, he's great like that. On the pitch, well, he is the guv'nor. He isn't just another foreign import, he's one of the greatest players the world has seen over the last ten years and it shows. He is teaching players so much, just by watching him, let alone playing with him.'

George Weah, World Footballer of the Year for 1996 paid his own tribute: 'I first met Ruud when we both played for the Rest of the World XI in Munich. He was very pleasant and respectful – a most decent man. When I met him he spoke to me like a son or a brother. He was full of encouragement and came across as a superb role model for us all. I really admire him as a player. Like Eric Cantona, Ruud always speaks the truth. He never hides from it and that has earned him huge respect worldwide. Without doubt, he's a superb player.'

Ruud reflected on his first season in the Premiership in an interview in the May 1996 edition of the authoritative *World Soccer*. 'I didn't know what to expect after Italy, but I was pleased to adapt so quickly. Things have gone better than I expected, but then I never expect too much. I just wanted to settle down and try to play my normal game. I really enjoy playing here. Sometimes in Italy you couldn't enjoy the game. Teams playing against Milan, for instance, get everyone back in defence and aim for 0–0. So they stay back and try to hang on. It's hard work breaking that down. Some games were fun, but there were many that were really tough. Mind you, there is nothing wrong in winning 1–0, even if the crowd give you the slow hand clap while you're doing it. The game in England is more open, which I enjoy. The Italian way helped me become more professional and was very good for me, but being in England is good for me, too. The style of play here is different to that in Holland and Italy, with lots of speed. But teams like Manchester United and Liverpool don't always play the traditional English style. They want to keep the ball and build their moves. I have been impressed by the quality of players here. Every team that Chelsea play has some really good players.'

Gullit enjoyed as startling a first season in English football as Jurgen Klinsmann did for Spurs. But Ruud will be around for longer than the German World Cup star in his new role as Chelsea player-manager after Glenn Hoddle's departure to the FA. At peace in his luxury apartment off Sloane Square, close to the King's Road, Ruud says: 'I like it. I had a wonderful feeling here, right from day one. I go out with friends and I like to see the black community. There are not many black people in Italy and it's marvellous to be among mixed races again; a bit like the Leiseplein district of Amsterdam, where all sorts of people mix together. There is much to see in London, and you have a lot of freedom, although I'm not a typical tourist. I play a lot of golf. My family like life here, too, and we have adapted well. If you speak English, there is no problem.'

Ruud's integration was so swift and smooth that he was the natural successor to Glenn Hoddle at the Bridge. A new extended contract as player-manager until June 1998, with an option for a year-by-year roll-on, ensures he will be a more permanent part of the English football scene than most high-profile foreign imports.

'I think England and Holland are very similar,' says Ruud, 'in terms of the weather and the kinds of people – but London has something special. I feel at ease walking around London and can go shopping without being mobbed all the time, which is very different to how things were at AC Milan. I also enjoy the company of the Chelsea players. I hope that as manager, my relationship with them won't change.'

Now that he has settled in London, Ruud will no doubt continue to frequent one of his favourite haunts outside of football – the nightclub. He remembers one particular episode from his time on the dancefloor: 'I was dancing in this disco one night when this very small, fat man came up to me and started hugging me. I thought it was a fan until his bodyguard came over. Then I recognised him. It was Diego Maradona.'

CHAPTER ONE

'I'm not a foreigner – I'm a world traveller'

Ruud Gullit loves to talk. He is knowledgeable on a wide range of subjects, of which football is not top of the list. But he doesn't just talk for the sake of it. He sees himself as a teacher and nothing seems to give him greater pleasure than an appreciative audience. He likes nothing better than to impart his wealth of knowledge about the game to others, whether they are team-mates or journalists. In his company I have been riveted by his wide range of subjects – including adoption, surrogate mothers, and environmental issues. Ruud would rather switch on the television to watch a fascinating documentary than bore himself with an uninteresting football match.

I followed Jurgen Klinsmann's one and only glory season in English football and there are numerous similarities. There are also some stark contrasts. The smiling German symbolised English soccer, season 1994/95. Every magazine, newspaper, radio and television programme featured Jurgen's endearing features. The World Cup star came to English football with a reputation of diving, but he did the right things, said the right things, smiled, and won the hearts and minds of the footballing nation. But after a while Klinsmann's interviews seemed to merge into one. Then he 'buggered off', as Alan Sugar put it succinctly, after just one season, and the Spurs chairman raised suspicions about the German's motives. Things came to a head during an interview for BBC's *Sportsnight* programme, when Sugar threw Klinsmann's Tottenham shirt to the floor in disgust.

Whether or not Klinsmann came for the money and to rekindle a diminishing career, the Premiership felt it would be poorer for the loss of the Football Writers' Footballer of the Year. But the following season, Gullit and many more foreign stars arrived to play in the Premier League.

When the news of Gullit's free transfer move from Sampdoria broke in the summer of 1995, there was the usual media speculation about the salary he would be earning in England. It was believed his original two-year deal with Chelsea amounted to around £1.6 million, a sum which would prove to be a bargain for the club, as the wages were spread over the duration of his two-year commitment without any transfer fee, at a time when prices were soaring. And now they have a new manager as well as a player for virtually the same amount of money.

When Gullit first arrived at the Bridge, Ken Bates recalls how money was the last thing on the Dutchman's mind. 'I'll tell you a little secret about Ruud which sums up the man perfectly. Ruud had been at the club a couple of months and he still hadn't bothered to open an English bank account. Colin Hutchinson called him over and said to him: "I've got your wage cheques here." Ruud told him, "Don't worry, Colin, you're my banker. Keep the cheques in the drawer until I need them!"

'He's got a lovely dry sense of humour. He is also very polite and respectful. One match day he spotted me before the game at my table and came over. I looked up at his dreadlocks and got out a comb. He just burst out laughing.

'Ruud is really the perfect diplomat. He never puts a foot wrong. The only trouble he's experienced occurs when he's been misquoted. His influence goes much deeper than the superficial.

There was annoyance within the club when he first joined that Gullit was the superstar and the rest didn't matter and that they were not good enough. It was patently untrue, but it hurt. Then, when Gullit was injured, the team won as many games without him as they did when he was in the team. That's not belittling his contribution in any way. In fact it's a compliment to him because it reflects his overall influence on the team whether he is playing or not. The truth is that Gullit was largely responsible for helping Glenn to get the younger players around to the manager's way of thinking.'

But there is not a hint of indulgence at the Bridge. Ruud works as hard as anyone in training and on the pitch. His influence has been immense, his sincerity unquestioned. A testimony to his sheer genius came from Glenn Hoddle. Despite Ruud's phenomenal success in Italy and with Holland, the former Chelsea boss detects that he is now playing some of the best football of his life.

'He is enjoying his football. In this game you learn by example. The players are watching him, playing with him and becoming better because of him. We signed Ruud as a sweeper, but later in the season we moved him into midfield and a lot of that credit has to go to David Lee. He took over as sweeper and did well. Then we started getting the ball to Ruud as quickly as possible. In some games in England, midfield can be like a tennis match. But we tried to build from the back and get it to Ruud and that allows him to go and influence the play. I knew he had another three years in him when I signed him. He is fit, got the talent and is still in love with the game. While he's got that, he is going to be a big influence at any club.'

His influence on players like Newton, Myers, Duberry, Sinclair and Furlong grew more important as the months went by and they got to know him better. Bates pointed out: 'His total unawareness of colour has made a great impression on our black players, particularly the young ones.' Ruud has always been outspoken on issues of racism in soccer, and attended the FA backed 'Kick Racism Out of Soccer' campaign just a couple of months after arriving in England.

Although it is widely assumed that Ruud is more effective in midfield, his first awards came as a result of his superb displays as a sweeper. *Mirror Sport* readers voted him the FA Premier League Crisps Most Valuable Player of the Month for September. He was also the first McDonald's/Shoot Player of the Month, averaging 8.25 ratings for his performances, including five man-of-the-match nominations in his first eight games. *Shoot* said: 'He was awarded a mark of nine out of ten in four of those great games and was head and shoulders above the rest of the Premiership stars.'

But you will never meet a more modest chap. When he was awarded the Evening Standard's Player of the Month award for January – as an outstanding midfield player – the newspaper's chief football correspondent Michael Hart, hardened by years in the cynical world of this particular tainted sport, was almost shocked by Gullit's reaction. He wrote: 'You would think that someone who has touched the heights of the world game might not rank winning the Evening Standard Footballer of the Month award too highly among the golden moments of an epic career. Yet Ruud Gullit turned out to be one of the most gracious recipients of the last quarter of a century. Not just gracious, but genuinely grateful. "I couldn't have won this without the rest of the team," he said. "They make a lot of jokes about me in the dressing room but I'm very happy with the guys." To prove the point, he insisted on including the rest of the Chelsea team in the photograph and publicly thanked his colleagues who have come to appreciate the enduring influence, at the age of 33, of one of the world's great players. "The first thing you want is that the team plays well," said Gullit. "A team is like a clock. If you take one piece out, it doesn't work".'

Gullit has become a born-again player since arriving at Chelsea. 'I seem to have gone back in time. I'm playing like it's the beginning of my career again and that I'm an 18-year-old again. The child in me can play on because I am still enjoying it, and if I enjoy it I can express myself better.' He also much prefers the attacking style of play over here compared to the often negative attitude back in Italy. 'In England you don't just stay back and defend,' he says. 'You are not a slave to tactics and results.'

To watch Gullit's long-range passing is a delight. It used to be the hallmark of Hoddle himself, but somehow Gullit has a far greater degree of consistency in his passing. That is what should be meant by the long ball, instead of the kick and rush, or kick and hope. Gullit plays the short passes with carefree simplicity and the long-range missiles with uncanny accuracy. As Michael Hart wrote: 'Gullit's job, wherever he plays, is quite simple. His presence, his ability on the ball, his vast stride, his vision, his range of passing ... all were essential to Hoddle's doctrine. With Gullit in the side the Chelsea players had the conviction they needed to successfully interpret Hoddle's tactics.'

A huge debate erupted during the course of the 1994/95 season over the value of imported stars, their quality and the influx as a result of the Bosman case. Gordon Taylor, of the Professional Footballers Association, was at the sharp end of the controversy with work permit problems involving Romanian World Cup star Ilie Dumitrescu. While Taylor is a concerned Euro-sceptic, he welcomed Klinsmann and laid down the red carpet for players like Gullit, Ginola, and Bergkamp. Their arrival, he believed, far from diminishing opportunities for home players that might be the case with the also-rans that join the influx, can stimulate young players' development. Taylor, nevertheless, insisted that while transfer turnover had now reached £130 million a year, the proportion of it going to clubs in the lower divisions was falling.

The desirability of too many foreign players was in question. But players of the highest quality can only enhance the English game and they don't come any higher than Ruud. As Stan Hey wrote in the *Independent on Sunday*: 'Gullit, whose magnificent physique and twirling dreadlocks are dramatic enough prologues even before he touches a ball, is probably the most prestigious import to the English game since Osvaldo Ardiles arrived at Tottenham with his World Cup winners' medal.'

The acquisition of Gullit was so natural for Hoddle after his decision to finally end his own illustrious playing career. Hoddle began his three-year stint as a player-manager at the Bridge in the sweeper role. He believed he had found the perfect player to fill the void. Hoddle, explaining the original concept for signing Gullit, said: 'I earmarked him three months before the end of the season when I was looking for a sweeper. The big question was whether we could get him. I thought at first it would be a struggle to afford him. Then, when I discovered he was on a free transfer, I couldn't believe it. It proved to be a long, hard struggle to get him here, but I am convinced it is going to be worthwhile struggle.'

Gullit's pre-requisite of any move from Italian football was the freedom to fulfil his desire to return to playing in a sweeper system. He was determined to make it work. But he equally accepted without complaint a switch to midfield where he became the cornerstone of Chelsea's transformation. Gullit was prepared to forsake his desire to play sweeper because of his respect and affection for Hoddle. Equally, Hoddle was ready to ditch his original conception of Gullit's role for the overall benefit of the team, yet still retain his philosophy of playing three at the back with David Lee taking over as the sweeper.

Right from the outset Gullit had an affinity with Hoddle as he explained at the start of the season: 'I like the way Glenn thinks about football. The reason I came to Chelsea is that it is one of the English clubs managed by an English player who has played abroad. Glenn Hoddle, like Kevin Keegan, wants more than just kick-and-rush football. Because if you keep possession of the ball, you can dictate the game, and wait for the right moment to attack. Most of the Premiership teams play more on the ball now, which is one of the reasons the rest of Europe has become so positive about the English game. If we have the ball, we can play to our own rhythm, rather than allow our opponents to play the ball at high speed. If you always have the ball, you can direct the game.'

It only took a few games for Gullit to appreciate that the sweeper role in English football would not be permanent. Gullit was never going to be dictatorial about his role as he explained from the very outset: 'In my career, coaches and managers have always tried to play me in different positions. I happen to be a player who can play in almost every position. Sometimes that's a bonus, sometimes it can be a disadvantage. I can say I claim the sweeper position for the entire season, but if we get problems up front I might be asked to go and play there.

'When I started playing as a kid it was as a libero because I was big and kicked very hard,' he said. 'I played there when I turned professional, but my club always needed someone strong up front. I went up front, made a lot of goals, which was my fault I know, then they needed someone on the right wing. I did well on the right wing, then PSV wanted me as a libero and I did well there. Then they needed someone up front, so I played up front and made goals – and so it has carried on.'

Ruud absorbs a great deal of information and has a wide range of interests. Unlike the archetype footballer whiling away those hours of free time watching football videos, drinking, betting or going to the dogs, Gullit has been hooked by the wide range of documentary programmes on television. After the second home match of the season, a thrilling, if disappointing 2–2 draw with Coventry, Gullit sat in the near deserted Bridge press room close to the dressing rooms discussing philosophy with a handful of journalists who could be bothered to wait until he had conducted an assortment of television and radio interviews. With a twelve-day break before the next match because of international games, Gullit was asked if he would indulge in catching up with English football by watching videos of matches. Not at all. Instead, he would continue his television diet of serious programmes. He said: 'I watch football on TV but not all the time. There are a lot more important things to see. Certain things are fascinating. One was about Siamese twins, and how the surgeons decided to separate them. One of the girls survives but misses her sister and even names her false leg after her twin. That touches you. You see what the children have to endure. You see the problems of autistic children and imagine how the parents have to live with it. Your whole life can be occupied by the plight of children. You see how lucky you are.

'Another was about a new cure for Parkinson's disease. I was watching this guy with his flailing arms and the surgeon drilling into his brain. You see the result, he is able to control himself and walk, and that is really something special. Things like this are the real world. You compare all this with what is happening to you. You can learn a lot about it. Football is part of life, but it is entertainment. There are other, more important things. These documentaries give you other aspects of life, something special, something emotional. Football doesn't rule my life.'

It was a remarkable insight into Ruud's perspective of life, as he was willing to talk endlessly about his innermost feelings when he watched those documentaries. He seemed less inclined to open up about his football!

The new Premiership season kicked off with a fascinating portrait of Gullit in *The Times* by their chief soccer writer Rob Hughes. He wrote: 'In many ways, Gullit is the symbol of what is happening to the English game in this hot, lazy, crazy summer. We are no longer buying cheap imports from eastern Europe, but men of character, status, achievement.'

However, *The Times* article posed pointed questions about Gullit's fitness, and desire. 'Does he arrive here too late, and diminished after the fearful injuries to his knees, the two failed marriages so ruthlessly exposed by the paparazzi?'

Gullit answered it straight away with an impeccable debut in the Premiership and withit the promise of real success for Chelsea after such a long wait. Goals were hard to come by at the start of the season for the Blues, but Gullit was their most effective player – in defence, midfield and attack!

Hoddle is convinced that Ruud can go on for another five years at the top. He has already seen enough to suggest that Gullit is as fit as ever. He says: 'There is no reason why he cannot go on until he is 37 or 38. Some people have been surprised by how fit he is, but I am not. I wouldn't have bought him if I hadn't done my homework. He is a real professional and looks after his body. Only people who love the game can play until that age. He knows that when he hangs up his boots he can abuse his body all he wants then. But while he loves the game and looks after himself, he has the vision to play on for years to come.'

Gullit adapted quickly to the contrast in philosophies from Italian football. So quickly that any thought of a culture shock was instantly dismissed. While he praises the game over here for a variety of reasons, he is critical of standards of the English game in Europe and world football. 'The Italian game is based on winning. How you win is unimportant. Here, the game is far more open and exciting and people all over the world love to watch it. But you don't win anything. The records show that and it was proved again last season. I love the game in England, but its future depends on the coaches. They have to make a choice.'

In his first season in English football, the prominent club sides failed miserably in Europe. Yet again the English League champions had failed to get past the first stage of the Champions League. Gullit observed: 'Since I've been here I've seen some good teams, but I'm surprised they still struggle in Europe. Sometimes they forget that teams are like cars, they have five gears, but some teams play in fourth and fifth gear all the time. You need to start off in first gear to get things moving. Liverpool can play in different gears. In Europe you have to learn patience. The English game is fast, the idea is to play the ball as quickly as possible into the box. In Europe, they play another game and English clubs may need to adapt themselves. And that will require more training and thinking about it.'

After a virtuoso performance at Loftus Road, as Chelsea beat QPR in the fourth round of the FA Cup, Gullit wandered into the Press Room where he gave another insight into his footballing philosophy. He revealed that he could see the transformation at the Bridge taking shape. 'All credit to Glenn for this, he wants to try and play football the way it should be played. The crowd are beginning to appreciate this keep-ball. At first, they would boo if you sent the ball backwards, but sometimes it had to go backwards to find areas to go forwards. We have to depend on our skills, but we can improve still further. We have to be more cynical [he meant 'clinical'] and we've not got that yet. To reach the top of our capabilities we have to be more cynical in front of goal, but it is good that we are learning what we have been doing wrong.'

In the vital Cup tie at QPR, Hoddle turned to Gullit as his captain for the first time in the absence of the suspended Dennis Wise. Gullit said: 'That was an honour on for me. The gaffer came to me and said, "I want to make you captain." I said OK.' The soccer cliché 'gaffer' seems to come naturally to Gullit, totally integrated with his team-mates. He said: 'I was never made captain in all my time in Milan. Never.'

Ruud has the potential to become anything he sets his mind to. He has embraced plenty of environmental issues during his years but dismisses the idea that he may one day go into politics. 'You have people without scruples in politics,' he said. 'They go with the wind. But it's not just politicians who are responsible for the world. It is all of us. You know, football is a game of 90 minutes. When it is over you return to the real life. There are many things in life other than football.'

Whatever the future holds, for the present Ruud Gullit is captivating fans and pundits alike. Anyone privileged to be in his company for an interview cannot help but come away with a warm inner glow. At last, we have a player without a chip on his shoulder, a diabolical disciplinary record, or the inability to express himself.

Clive White, in an article for the *Sunday Telegraph*, observed: 'A few minutes spent in Gullit's company is enough to make one realise that here is a man in pursuit of excellence, whether it be for the betterment of himself or his team, rather than some monetary goal.'

Gullit's stature and class have never been questioned. And, once he established his commitment to English football, and produced near perfect performances in virtually every game in which he played for Chelsea, some of the more respected pundits began to warm to him even more.

Brian Glanville, in his analysis of the glut of foreign players, wrote in the *Sunday People*: 'Supreme among them all of course is Ruud Gullit, even if his age and those knee operations mean you can't expect him to run around for 90 minutes. But Gullit is so much more than a schemer – he's "total football" personified. Sweeper, striker, midfielder: call him what you will. What he proves, game by game, is that a player with high technique and real imagination is worth his weight in gold.'

However, Gullit doesn't consider himself to be a foreigner. 'I'm not a foreigner,' he says. 'I'm a world traveller.'

CHAPTER TWO

Rebuilding the Bridge

It was a decision from the heart. That's how Ruud described his reason for leaving Italy for Stamford Bridge. Money was not the motivating factor. A multi-millionaire in his own right, there were even greater fortunes on offer to ply his still considerable talents in Japan, France and Turkey. Instead he chose one last glory trail in the Premiership, pledging that his knees are no longer a problem, the rest of his body is in sublime condition and that he's ready for the physical conflict.

Gullit explained his decision at the time: 'The choice I made was with the heart instead of the head. I wasn't thinking about money. I was thinking as a player, not a businessman. I needed a fresh challenge as a football player and that is why I was interested in coming to England. In my eight years in Italy, I never thought I'd ever play in England. I had won everything I wanted to win in Italy and I wanted to end my career there, but things happened which changed that. I had some interesting offers, but when Glenn called me, I knew I had to take up this challenge.

'I felt at home in England from the very first day. I've never experienced anything like that before. I love the language, the way the people treat you, and everything else is so much similar to life in Holland. And, it's so close to Holland. I was brought up in the city of Amsterdam. Amsterdam is cosmopolitan and so is

London. I like the life of the city and for me, Chelsea is a very nice part of London.'

Gullit has always had an affinity for the English game. 'I had the chance to come to England at the beginning of my career, but I felt I was too young. I can't remember which club wanted me ... I think it was Leeds.' In fact Spurs, Arsenal and Ipswich were also very interested.

Gullit might even have played in the same side as Hoddle at Spurs. Peter Shreeves, the then Spurs coach and later assistant to Hoddle at the Bridge, did his best to take Gullit to White Hart Lane in 1984. Shreeves recalls: 'One of my tasks at Spurs was to prepare a file on European opposition. When we drew Feyenoord I saw this boy playing sweeper and I thought he was just magnificent. I came back to the club and told manager Keith Burkinshaw that I had just seen one of the most exciting young players around. It just so happened that I went over to Dublin to watch Chris Hughton play for the Republic of Ireland, and there was this Dutch winger flying past him. Now, I knew how quick Chrissie was, so this player had to be pretty fast to do that. And, it turned out to be the same player I had seen as the Feyenoord sweeper.' Spurs made a big effort to sign Gullit but Shreeves pointed out: 'His agent didn't think it was the right time for him to move abroad, and he was probably quite right.'

Chelsea's quest for Gullit began early in 1995 when Hoddle was already plotting ahead to rebuild his side. He had been a long standing admirer of Gullit and was hot on his trail from the second he became aware he was available on a free transfer from Sampdoria. It was in a UEFA Cup tie back in 1984 that Hoddle first encountered Gullit in a match. It was a clash against Feyenoord where one of Hoddle's heroes, Johan Cruyff, was coming to the end of his illustrious career. Hoddle recalls: 'Ruud was a youngster. I was playing for Spurs when we knocked

Feyenoord out of Europe. He was used as a sweeper that day and he was also in the same position when we played against PSV Eindhoven in a pre-season friendly a couple of years later. I recall his wonderful reading of the game, his passing and anticipation. Even at that age he could run the match. It made a big impression on me and, of course, I have watched and admired his career ever since.'

On Friday 19 May 1995, Hoddle made a whistle-stop tour of Italy in his quest to link up Paul Gascoigne, then unsettled at Lazio, with Gullit. The Chelsea boss flew directly from a meeting with Gazza in Rome to Milan, where he met the Dutch star. The meeting with Hoddle was one of like minds. Hoddle wanted a dominant sweeper and was shocked when he discovered that Gullit wanted precisely that role.

Hoddle recalled that first meeting. 'I had played against him, nodded to him after matches, but had never met Ruud. That first meeting was to make contact. We talked football, and I told him where I wanted him to play and what I expected from Chelsea. We returned home without any assurances, but then I began to hear there might be a chance we could get him. I was desperate to keep it quiet, which is not easy these days.'

Chief executive Colin Hutchinson accompanied Hoddle on his Italian sojourn. Hutchinson said: 'Our No 1 target was always Ruud Gullit but we wanted Gazza as well. In fact, I was the first person to sit down with Lazio's Sergio Cragnotti and Dino Zoff and we agreed a fee of £4.25 million. Then we spoke to Gascoigne's advisors Len Lazarus and Mel Stein and agreed a deal on personal terms. But the key to it was always going to be Paul himself. We always prefer to sit down with the player first, to gauge his ambitions and find out if he really wants to play for Chelsea. But this time it all happened the opposite way around.

'Glenn and myself talked things over with Gazza over a meal.

He was polite and friendly and we joked a little – especially when Gazza swallowed the crown to his tooth that he had just had fitted! But I came away from the meeting feeling that Gazza did not really want to play for Chelsea.

'The next day we had made secret arrangements to go to Milan to see Gullit. But that morning Glenn and I saw an Italian newspaper and although neither of us know much Italian, we knew enough to read that it said Gullit was about to sign for Chelsea. We had arranged to meet him at the AC Milan offices at 4 pm but when we got there it was swarming with Press men. We met an agent there and he sent us to a nearby hotel and then on to another agent's office. But there was still no sign of Gullit. We told them that if we didn't see him shortly then they could forget the deal. At 5 pm we were back at the AC Milan offices and when Glenn and I walked through the door, Ruud was already there.

'I asked, "Who are we negotiating with?", meaning agents and he replied, "Just me." I thought that was a refreshing change. In that meeting we spoke about nothing but football, no money was even discussed, unlike with Gazza. His enthusiasm for the game came over and all he wanted to know was about Chelsea, how Glenn wanted the side to play and how Glenn wanted him to play. He asked for time to think it over and a few days later rang Glenn to say he wanted to talk further. We flew to Milan in secret a week later and had a two-hour meeting where we discussed terms and made him our best offer.

'We knew we were certainly not making him the best financial offer. Ruud could have gone to Japan and earned £3 million a year. But he was interested in the football side rather than the money. And our biggest advantage was that he got on so well with Glenn. There was a mutual respect there. So, even though we knew he could earn a lot more money elsewhere, we always felt fairly confident of signing him.'

Gascoigne, meanwhile, had not made up his mind where to go after Italy. Gazza said: 'I have spoken to Chelsea, Aston Villa and Glasgow Rangers. I've heard rumours about Leeds and I think I will speak to them next week.' He eventually opted to switch to Scottish football, accepting a mega-offer from wealthy Rangers .

With Gullit available on a free transfer, there were clubs all around the world interested in his signature. Bryan Robson and Ray Wilkins entered the battle with their old England pal Hoddle. Wilkins said: 'Don't believe all this clap-trap that he is over the hill. Gullit is a very fit man. I had the privilege of playing against him for AC Milan when he was with PSV Eindhoven. Ironically, when he arrived at AC Milan, he took my place!' Gullit's preference to return to the sweeper role he made famous at the start of his career did not bother Wilkins: 'I don't care where he plays, he can even have a turn out in goal if he likes, I just want him here at this club.'

Hoddle knew Gazza was Glasgow Rangers bound, which made him all the more determined to land Gullit, particularly as Graeme Souness, then the newly installed manager of Turkish side Galatasaray, moved in for Gullit, with an offer on the table of £1 million-a-year in wages.

But Gullit turned his back on all of these offers, with the moment the whole of Chelsea had been waiting for coming on Bank Holiday Monday, 29 May 1995. Colin Hutchinson recalls: 'I was just settling down to watch the Bolton-Reading play-off final, when Ruud called. By the time we had finished talking, Reading were 2–0 up and Gullit had agreed to sign. One of the reasons behind his decision, he said, was that Chelsea played in white socks – and he had always won things playing for teams who wore white socks!

'Glenn was halfway across the Atlantic at the time, on his way to Florida for a holiday. I had to ring his hotel and leave a coded message for him saying, 'The man from Italy has said, yes'. He was delighted.'

Hoddle left the final details to Hutchinson. 'The second time we went over, the deal was done,' says Hoddle. 'We discovered Ruud wanted to play in English football and he wanted to play for Chelsea. Every side needs someone like Ruud Gullit, a player who can win a game with one pass, a player who is a cut above the rest and a player who can hurt the opposition by doing what comes naturally.'

Hutchinson made one of the most fruitful, exciting and profitable journeys of his life when he travelled to Milan to complete the deal for Gullit on Tuesday, 30 May 1995. He said: 'I flew out to Genoa to meet Gullit's lawyer and draft the contract. The following day I met up with the lawyer and Ruud once again. Within ten minutes he had said 'yes'. I had just completed arguably the biggest deal ever done in British football. I took out my camera and asked the lawyer to take a picture of me with Ruud to capture the moment. We went out for lunch and while we were eating an agent rang Ruud on his mobile phone and said that Tottenham and QPR were interested in signing him. I had a smile to myself because I already had his signature.

'Then I flew home via Frankfurt. At Frankfurt airport I sat next to a Leyton Orient fan and we got talking and he asked me what I did. I told him and said I had just signed Gullit for Chelsea. Then two English bricklayers came and sat by us and one was saying how he had just telephoned a friend to pick him up at the airport. He said his mate was an Arsenal fan and was winding him up that Chelsea had signed Ruud Gullit. And the Orient fan turned to him and said, 'That's no wind-up – and here's the man who has done the deal'. I just sat there grinning and feeling absolutely fantastic.'

Chelsea had successfully fought off counter-bids from

Galatasaray, Bayern Munich, the club Jurgen Klinsmann joined from Spurs, Hoddle's former French club Monaco, and Gullit's old club Feyenoord, plus a number of Japanese teams which offered him a fortune, notably Yokohama Flugels.

Diplomatically Gullit would not divulge why he rejected the other offers. He explained: 'I enjoy life every day and I never take decisions for a long period. I always follow my instinct, which has rarely misled me. My old club Feyenoord would have liked to have me back. But the city of London appealed more to me than the port of Rotterdam. But the real reason for not joining Feyenoord, Galatasaray or any of the other clubs who knocked on my door this summer, I will not tell. Whatever I say will be wrong in the fans' eyes and in the opinion of people who play for those clubs. As soon as Chelsea turned up on my doorstep and I had met Glenn Hoddle, I knew I wanted to go an play at Stamford Bridge.'

Chelsea knew that gates would soar and commercial spin-offs would follow. Hutchinson said: 'We wanted a player who would put bums on seats and we have certainly got that. And, remember, he has not cost us a single penny in terms of a transfer fee.' In London, Gullit mania was instant. Hutchinson said: 'On the day of the announcement, the reaction from the fans was incredible. The switchboard at Stamford Bridge was jammed, there was a queue of thirty-five people at the club's shop that morning when it opened. People wanted to buy shirts and have Gullit's name put on them. Requests for membership forms and season tickets are coming in thick and fast so his magic is already working.'

The Chelsea players, much the same as their fans, were staggered by the signing of Gullit. Scott Minto was sunning himself in Gran Canaria, when he caught up with the news. 'A couple of days before we actually signed him, a few people had been coming up to us and talking about it, saying we were going to get him. We had read a few things in the papers but it sounded a bit ridiculous and we didn't take much notice of it at the time. Then I rang home and my mum said: 'Did you know they've just signed Ruud Gullit?' Because she doesn't know anything about the game or who he is, I knew she wasn't making it up. Then someone else rang home to check and we found out it was true. It took a little while to sink in but we all thought it was brilliant.'

When Chelsea club captain and England international Dennis Wise escaped a three-month jail sentence on 2 June, he talked about his relief that he will be teaming up with Gullit rather than starting the season in jail. A judge overturned his convictions for attacking a taxi driver and damaging his cab. Wise said later: 'I want to put it all behind me and get on with the rest of my career. I am happy and am going on holiday fairly shortly. I will be all right for the beginning of the season, when we've got Ruud Gullit to look forward to.'

Brian Glanville devoted his *Sunday People* column to Chelsea's new player. He wrote: 'Ruud Gullit's signing for Chelsea is a tremendous coup for the Stamford Bridge club. Even today, at the age of 32, after all those fearful operations on his right knee, Gullit is among the few great players in the world. Fans will come to see him. There's no doubt at all about his ability to play as sweeper as he demonstrated in his early years with Feyenoord. It's really just a question of whether the Chelsea team will be able to adjust to the somewhat unfamiliar tactics ... He shouldn't find it too hard to work with Hoddle, and the younger Chelsea players will surely learn from him. Let's just hope he stays longer in London than Jurgen Klinsmann.'

The boardroom split between chairman Ken Bates and club director Matthew Harding even managed to involve Gullit. Bates pointed out that he authorised the acquisition of Gullit without Harding's millions to back him up. Bates said: 'We proved what a solid financial concern Chelsea is with the signing of Ruud Gullit, one of the biggest names in world soccer. It was all financed from within the club's budget, without having to ask Matthew Harding or anyone else for a single penny.'

In the first week of June, Gullit fulfilled his final commitments with Sampdoria on a tour of Hong Kong and China, a popular destination for many leading clubs in the summer. It also enabled Gullit to combine the football with four days of highly lucrative promotional work in Japan. Back in London, Ken Bates was airing his plans for a floatation of Chelsea. With the signing of Gullit on a reputed £16,000 a week, Mr Bates joked: 'We need a flotation to help pay his wages!'

The Dutch revolution in English football continued when Dennis Bergkamp signed for Arsenal. Bergkamp became hooked on Spurs, and in particular their midfield maestro Glenn Hoddle, from the moment he saw them on Dutch television as a five-year-old. Bergkamp revealed: 'I had only one idol when I was young and that was Glenn Hoddle. My family went on holiday to England one year and we visited White Hart Lane. My dad bought me a Spurs strip and a mug with the crest on it. Every year after that I would get a new Spurs strip and it always had to have Glenn's number on it. He was the reason I supported them. He was such a wonderful player. When I played football with my mates out on the street it would always be an FA Cup Final with Tottenham in it and I, of course, would be Hoddle. I still have a soft spot for them and look for their results every week.'

On Thursday, 22 June, Gullit arrived in London, jet lagged from his worldwide travels. The formalities of his Chelsea signing were completed, including the routine medical which he passed with ease. The next day he breezed into the Bridge at precisely 11:04 am to a barrage of cameras in Drakes restaurant, which snuggles neatly inside the new £5 million stand.

A year earlier Jurgen Klinsmann had re-launched his career and re-established his worldwide reputation in English football. Gullit arrived with the same steely-eyed approach. He said: 'I'm hungry for this new challenge. My ambitions at first are quite simple, they are to get along with the lads and adapt to my new environment, a different lifestyle, different customs, a different way of life. I'm not thinking about any end result yet. I am very satisfied that I have done the right thing. My knee problems are a thing of the past. I know there were plenty of rumours about my knees last year but I feel frustrated that I couldn't prove them wrong with Sampdoria. All those problems are in the past. Milan said I couldn't play three matches in a week. But they never gave me the chance. Right now, I have never felt fitter.'

Gullit is synonymous with extravagant goals but revealed he never had any intention of playing attacking roles. He said: 'When I got to Milan, the coach, Saachi, wanted me to play as a striker. He just told me, 'Go out there and just do your best'. But it's not natural for me, and it's not somewhere I prefer to play, although I learnt a lot from doing it. I don't have a striker's instincts. A true striker kills every ball and wants to score every time. Sometimes I'm sloppy and try to do too much and miss the chance. A true striker has to be egocentric.'

From the moment Gullit arrived he charmed his audience in his typical relaxed mood. He never even faltered when he mistook Wimbledon for Wembley! Asked what he thought about the prospects of playing at Wimbledon he said: 'I'm looking forward to it, it's one of the most important stadiums in the world.' When his error was pointed out by Hoddle, who was sitting next to him, he laughed loudly at himself and said: 'Perhaps I should talk about tennis as well!'

Gullit answered every conceivable question, no matter how obscure or personal. It was hard to know whether to take him seriously or not when he gave a bizarre reason for why he chose Chelsea – the reason being that he'd always won things playing for teams who wore white socks! Finally, he politely paraded in a No 4 Chelsea shirt on the pitch where there were a succession of television interviews. He said: 'I had the choice between the number 4 and number 14 shirts. It's strange to see players wearing 18 or 19 because I don't think the public can identify with them, or know where they're really supposed to be playing. I prefer numbers that correspond with a player's position.'

There was also a first in Gullit's big unveiling to the Chelsea fans. Never before had one of Gullit's media introductions been sidetracked somewhat by the shock announcement of the signing of another player, Mark Hughes from Manchester United. But it was the surprise factor, more than anything else, that had the media contingent gasping.

Colin Hutchinson made the Hughes announcement just as Gullit was concluding his radio interviews. The Dutchman was immediately effusive. 'I'm delighted Hughes is coming,' he said. 'I think he's a great player. I know all about him, I played against him when he was at Barcelona. I knew that Glenn Hoddle wanted to sign him from the very start ... but I can keep a secret!'

I suggested to Hoddle that Hughes and Gullit, both into their thirties, are truly Chelsea pensioners. The Chelsea boss smiled and said: 'Both these guys are fit lads who have the right habits and attitudes. I found out myself, when I hung up my boots at the age of 37 going on 38, that people tell me it's too early. It's about quality, not about age, and these two guys certainly have the right pedigree. Perhaps I'd better sign a few fifteen year olds to balance it up!'

In fact, Hoddle believed that the capture of Gullit was a watershed in Chelsea's fortunes and helped to recruit Hughes. 'When you sign somebody like Ruud Gullit after all that he's achieved, it is sending out the right signals, to our own supporters first and to his team-mates. It says that people here are trying to build something, that they are serious. It says that we want to be one of the leading sides, that we want to win something. I've been here for two years and we've come close. But I'm not into transfer coups, I'm into trying to win trophies.'

In the light of the British record of £8.5 million splashed out on Stan Collymore, £6 million on Les Ferdinand, no spring chicken himself, and £4.5 million on Chris Armstrong, the capture of Hughes was an absolute steal. Hoddle said: 'Compared to the fees that are knocking around at the moment, it makes an awful lot of economic sense to sign Gullit on a free transfer and Hughes at the end of his contract for £1.5 million.'

The arrival of the two players was extremely well received by the media. Neil Harman, *Daily Mail* Football Correspondent, wrote: 'Not a dreadlock on his head turned when the Ruud Gullit interview was interrupted by news that Chelsea had signed Mark Hughes. His thunder might have been temporarily stolen but, in the best tradition of a world superstar, his stride-pattern remained unaffected.

'When you've spent the best part of 20 years as a supreme, sublime talent and cost a then world record transfer-fee of £5.5 million eight years ago, the small matter of a free to Chelsea is nothing to get seismic about. After a week in which London rivals Tottenham and Arsenal between them splashed out £12 million on strikers, Chelsea's double coup looks fair business ... His enticement from Italian football must be the best bit of business for many summers, even though there are those who say so much damage to priceless limbs has left Gullit with knees of glass.'

World Soccer reviewed the Gullit press conference. 'He made an impressive entry onto the platform, partnered by his new boss. Cracking jokes with the press, he was clearly confident in a foreign tongue. Rewind a year and this could have been Jurgen Klinsmann's debut before the British media.'

Chelsea reaped immediate benefits from their summer signings. Season tickets sales had beaten the previous year's figure. Usually, demand drops during the summer holiday period but sales were up with a steady flow of renewals and new applications. The club was forced to introduce a waiting list for fans wanting to pre-book tickets for forthcoming glamour matches. All but two of the club's twenty-four executive boxes had been sold and there had also been an increase in applications for the family section.

Hughes finalised his £1.5 million move from Manchester United on 5 July and confirmed that Gullit's arrival had convinced him to sign for Chelsea.

Hughes had met Gullit briefly on holiday a year earlier and they had faced each other in the international arena several times, but he never dreamed he would be lining up alongside him. 'The fact that Chelsea signed Ruud showed they were intent on raising their profile and I have always been at big clubs. It might have been difficult for me not playing to large crowds every week, but it looks as though we will be attracting the big gates home and away. Gullit is the complete footballer. Genuine world class, a player you can put anywhere in the side and he plays with presence and stature. A superstar.'

Gullit and Hughes were missing when Chelsea began pre-season training on Wednesday, 12 July. Hoddle agreed to give his new signings an extended break following club and country commitments. Gullit and Hughes turned up for training for the first time on Wednesday, 19 July, and the rest of the Chelsea players were in awe of their arrival. Scott Minto said: 'It was a bit like being at school when they were introduced. We were half way through the warm-up in training when Peter Shreeves came over with them and said: 'I'd like to introduce you all to Ruud Gullit and Mark Hughes.' That was all he said, really. They stood there, we looked at them and gave them a round of applause.'

CHAPTER THREE

Gullit Mania

Stamford Bridge was a building site. The underground car park was under construction and planks of wood were used as a walk way to cover the dirt, nails and general debris. Hardly the San Siro. But Gullit had now swapped Italian football for the Bridge. It was certainly a culture shock.

Ruud had no concept of the impact his arrival would have. It began to dawn on him on Friday, 28 July when nearly fifty fans waited for hours to catch a glimpse of Gullit as Chelsea held a photo-call followed by a training session. They were not to be disappointed. Even a little old lady managed to overcome the 'building site' and waited for five hours to find herself among the throng stationed patiently outside the dressing room area. Coach Peter Shreeves took the players through their paces in glorious sunshine with Gullit teaming up with his manager Glenn Hoddle, other new boy Mark Hughes and midfielder Nigel Spackman in one training group. 'It was nice and tough, quite hard, that's because Mark Hughes and myself started a week later than the rest,' said Gullit, 'I can tell I still have some catching up to do.' When Gullit emerged, the fans surged forward pleading for him to sign shirts, photographs, autograph albums or any piece of paper. He signed them all.

Carrying a bright coloured rucksack over his shoulders, under his arm the Italian *Gazetto dello Sport* and the *Dutch Telegraph*, he was perfectly relaxed as he surveyed the re-birth of the Bridge. He observed: 'Brilliant, isn't it? The place is really buzzing. I mean, the whole of English football is exploding and blossoming. Stadiums are being expanded, the fans turn up in their thousands, all the stars want to play in the Premier League. It could not be better for English football. That is why I want to enjoy what is happening here.'

In the club's reception area, Gullit practised his colloquial English on the telephonist. 'Can I make a phone call?' he asked in perfect Cockney. He told a Dutch journalist who had made the trek from Holland on the off-chance of an interview: ' I like the sound of the language here, I like to speak in English and I can pick it up quite quickly.' Proud of his grasp of the Cockney slang, he laughed out loud.

Once the crowd had dispersed, Gullit and one of the club's member of staff strolled down the Fulham Road and stopped for a snack at the newly opened Calzone Pizza Bar. A local, upper crust sounding, elderly gent with white handlebar moustache and shorts, held out his hand and said: 'Nice to see you here Mr Gullit, we are ever so glad you chose Chelsea.' Gullit smiled and politely said 'Thank you', and swaggered down Park Walk feeling very much at home in the Royal Borough of Chelsea.

The attitudes and reactions of the fans helped Ruud to settle down instantly. He said at the time: 'In Italy everyone is so obsessed about football that they try to own you and think nothing of coming up to you in a shop or in a restaurant in a group and crowding you for an autograph or a photo. In England, the people are much more dignified and they respect your space.'

As for the heat wave hitting London, he said: 'They told me about England … so much rain, wet pitches. So far it's been hotter than in Italy in my first few weeks here! I just love this weather.'

And, he was convinced that Hoddle was getting it right on the training ground. 'Glenn Hoddle knows how Chelsea must play in the Premier League to become a hit. He has organised the club very well and is running things almost perfectly. I was surprised to see that our training sessions are almost a copy of the ones at AC Milan. We do exactly the same things. Before I came here, I did not think any English club would train like they do.'

On Saturday, 22 July, the little non-league club Kingstonian had seen nothing like it. Director Matthew Harding turned up in a Chelsea shirt with Gullit's name on the back! Gullit and Hughes were presented to the King's Meadow crowd and the duo waved to the supporters. They got a great reception on their first public appearance together. Unfortunately for the 5,000 fans the club's new signings took their places in the stand to watch their opening pre-season game – Chelsea winning 5–0. They were not quite fit enough to play as assistant manager Peter Shreeves said: 'They are in the squad but haven't done enough training.' But the fact that they were there was enough, at half-time, for a Gullit lookalike to cause a pitch invasion of autograph hunters! Before the end Gullit left to avoid any crowd problems, with reserve team manager Graham Rix as his chauffeur.

Reminiscent of Jurgen Klinsmann's first appearance in a friendly at Vicarage Road, Watford, exactly a year earlier, it was near hysteria at Gillingham for the welcome of Ruud Gullit, on Tuesday, 25 July. Gullit lead out the team and took centre stage as he was chased by a posse of cameramen and eager autograph hunters who streamed on to the pitch. Four thousand Chelsea fans made the journey to watch Gullit and Hughes.

The gates were locked minutes after kick-off and hundreds of broken-hearted youngsters were led away in tears by disappointed dads. The luckier ones watched from windows and garage roofs overlooking the ground. Gullit was mobbed at every opportunity. The media interest overwhelmed a club that had finished three places from the bottom of the Endsleigh Third Division the season before. He tried to warm up as he signed autographs, and followed, like some footballing Pied Piper, by the adoring kids. He said: 'It is the first time in my entire career that I have played without being able to warm up. It seemed as if there were hundreds of fans around wherever I went.' And, with a flash of his wicked sense of humour he said: 'The people seemed to go mad ... I suppose that's what the papers describe as Gullit-mania!'

The capacity 10,425 Priestfield crowd witnessed Gullit strolling through his first 45 minutes in English football as Chelsea won 3–1. For the Kent club it was a massive pay day. Gullit might earn more in a week than a Gillingham player would earn in a year, but the club were loving the way the turnstiles never stopped clicking. The estimated £60,000 receipts brightened the life of a club that had faced extinction. Only four weeks earlier Gillingham was saved from bankruptcy after six months in receivership. New chairman Paul Scally, the Sevenoaks businessman who rescued the club, was delighted with the evening's takings. He said: 'That will pay the wages for July.'

When Gullit left the spectacular surroundings of *Serie A*, he probably never expected to pull on a Chelsea jersey for the first time at a ground that can boast the oldest stand in the League, built in 1899 by dockers for beer and cigarettes on their summer break. It's still there because the club cannot afford to replace it.

But here he was, starting his practise sessions in earnest as a sweeper. Flanked by Frank Sinclair and Erland Johnsen, Gullit was immediately in evidence, switching neatly with Nigel Spackman as he raced forward, abandoning defensive duties when he saw the opportunity to join the attack. The Dutchman conceded two early corners, and he would have been disappointed with himself with his first two shots. However, he soon got his aim, and his third shot, a cracking 30 yarder, forced a full length diving save from keeper Jimmy Glass after Gillingham had stolen the lead.

Chelsea's defence was embarrassed by the power of student Leo Fortune-West, a £5,000 buy from Stevenage, with the money paid by Gillingham fans. He put Andy Myers under pressure and the Chelsea left-back knocked the ball past Dmitri Kharine. Chelsea levelled when Mark Stein converted a penalty after Dennis Wise had been brought down.

Gullit stayed in the dressing room at half-time, needing treatment for blisters. Mark Hughes came on, to inspire a Chelsea victory with a virtuoso goal, dribbling past a bewildered defence before aiming low into the corner after 68 minutes. Chelsea made sure with a second penalty supplied by Gavin Peacock.

Afterwards Gullit said: 'I had never heard of Gillingham before coming here, but that did not matter, it was just good to play against a team which plays the English way. It was good to have a tough game. I've had hundreds of letters from supporters telling me how pleased they are that I have decided to sign for Chelsea. I have a great feeling about this move already. There are some good players at Chelsea and I am impressed. We have a team that is technically very good. The players have great skill and English football is changing. It is no longer kick and rush. I'm impressed with everything I have seen in this match and in training but we won't get carried away. Rome was not built in a day.'

The Chelsea fans got their first sight of Ruud at Stamford Bridge on Sunday, 30th July in a 1–1 draw with FC Porto for Paul Elliott's testimonial. Just as anticipated, the fans flocked to the Bridge wearing their brand new Gullit shirts. And, there were Gullit wigs on sale outside of the ground at £10 a time.

Porto manager Bobby Robson drooled over the conversion of

Gullit to the sweeper role. The former England manager, who took England to the World Cup semi-finals in Italy 1990, described Gullit as 'another Franz Beckenbauer'.

Apart from Gullit's class, the huge crowd were also treated to a stunning Hughes effort. Only five minutes had gone by when the Welshman jack-knifed to bludgeon a characteristic header into the net from Mark Stein's cross. Both Gullit and Hughes were substituted before the end. Gullit stayed on until 65 minutes and Hughes lasted until eight minutes before the end. Hoddle chose the occasion to give most of his squad a run-out, including himself, as he came on for the last 14 minutes.

With rebuilding work still taking place, the local council cut the ground capacity to 19,000, yet 16,689 turned out to witness Gullit and Hughes in their first home game. Elliott, whose career ended two years earlier in a tackle with Dean Saunders, had faced a legal bill for £500,000 after losing to the former Liverpool striker in court. Ladbrokes presented Elliott with a £500 bet on Chelsea winning the title at 40–1. But on Hoddle's own admission, Chelsea's best hope for a trophy was in one of the Cups. He was to be proved exactly right.

Testimonials at the Bridge have been notoriously poorly attended, even stars like Kerry Dixon attracted a meagre 5,000 fans. Colin Hutchinson said: 'Paul must have thought he'd won the national lottery when after arranging his game against Porto we went out and signed Gullit and Hughes.' The club handed over all the £250,000 receipts to Elliott. In addition, the player had the programme, advertising, and peripheral rights including a TV deal with Sky.

Two weeks later, Chelsea journeyed to Gullit's homeland to take on Feyenoord in their final pre-season friendly. Gullit was still not entirely happy with his game. He explained: 'I am still making mistakes, I need a few more 90 minutes under my belt to get things right. We have eased through pre-season without too much trouble, so maybe we need to lose a game before we begin the season in earnest. We will be better for it, and will all learn from it. You don't really know how well you are doing until you have tasted defeat.'

The team arrived on Thursday evening in Rotterdam, on 11th August. They engaged in light training, returned to the hotel and then Ruud took the opportunity to re-acquaint himself with some of the night spots in the city. He said: 'I needed a little break, and it's so nice to comeback to the town where it all started for me. I have seen a lot of my old friends.'

The tears flowed for Ruud as he made an emotional return to his old club on the Saturday. He was guest of honour at the opening of Feyenoord's superbly refurbished stadium. A crowd of 38,000 turned out to see his 'homecoming' at the ground where he forged his reputation.

But there were two very unexpected 'fans' who brought the big man to his first burst of tears. The Chelsea team coach arrived at the ground at 6.30 pm for the 8.15 kick-off and as the player disembarked from the bus Gullit's eyes met two little girls ... his daughters from his first marriage, Felicity and Sharmayne. His former wife, Yvonne, stood in the background as the two girls were delighted to see their father. It was a total surprise for Ruud. He was extremely emotional with the reunion, but at the same time deeply annoyed that the TV cameras and Dutch media were present to record a very private event. His two girls watched the match, and so did Ruud's mum. After the match, the girls presented Ruud with a drawing of him inscribed 'Our dad is the best.' The only English newspaper to refer to this touching moment was *The Times* a week or so later. Rob Hughes wrote: 'He protects those girls from every contact with the media, with football, with the publicity that is essential to his and their wealth.'

There was another highly charged moment for Ruud, when during the warm up he was presented with a special presentation in his honour. A leading Dutch journalist explained: 'The chances are that this was his final game on Dutch soil as he will never play again for his the national team and Chelsea are sure to be his last big club. The last time he played here he was booed and whistled because he had just walked out of the Dutch camp and refused to play for Holland. Everyone now feels it was a terrible way to say goodbye and wanted to rectify that for such a great player.'

Leading Dutch celebrity Koos Postema, the Terry Wogan of Holland and a very close friend of Ruud, gave him a big kiss as he made the presentation. Ruud was handed the microphone and made a speech to the crowd. He was applauded for a full ten minutes! When he took the microphone the crowd sang 'You'll Never Walk Alone' and there was another bout of tears.

Ruud told the crowd: 'I am so surprised and honoured and flattered. I am so proud that you the public, in the city where all the big things started to happen for me, are doing this. It means so much. With Feyenoord I won my first championship, and won the double. It was the club I met the two biggest characters in football, Johan Cruyff and Wim van Hanegem. That's why this club will always be special to me and why I will keep this club close to my heart for the rest of my life. Whether I'll return to this club as a player, I don't know. My future, as you all know, is in England. I hope Feyenoord do well. I honestly wish them all the luck in the world.'

Ruud put on a five-star show but got the defeat he asked for! The Dutchman sprayed his long range passes all over the field, but Chelsea's new continental system failed to click. Gullit almost inspired Chelsea to take the lead. Mark Stein sped away behind the Feyenoord defence to pick up a glorious Gullit pass but, instead of picking out Mark Hughes, he flashed the ball across the face of the goal. A 40 yard Gullit pass early in the second half enabled Andy Myers to cross for Gavin Peacock, whose diving header was just wide. Then Gullit picked out Stein whose cross for Hughes was wasted. The game was settled in the 68th minute with a goal from Feyenoord's Orlando Trustfull.

After the game Ruud told journalists: 'Chelsea is a bigger challenge than any other club could have given me after eight years in Italy. I am still very ambitious and Chelsea have not won anything for a long time. It would excite me, tremendously, if I could get things going there and win a major trophy. It would follow the same pattern at the other clubs I have joined.'

Ruud was cautious on the eve of his Premiership debt. He labelled his new Chelsea team-mates his 'virgin' soldiers and warned the Stamford Bridge fans not to let their dreams run away with them. His priority at the outset was all about setting standards and reaching them. For him, victories could wait. It was more about playing well, not so much about winning well. He explained: 'If we don't win it is not so important, there will be other games to win. In England there are so many games, so many demands! So many things could happen but what you can be sure of is that the season will be full of ups and downs. We won't win every game.

'The secret of a successful team is to stay calm and retain your belief. To keep a cool head when the pressure is on from either the fans, the press or the chairman. We have a good team at Chelsea but we are a young team. If you like, we are virgins, still getting to know each other. My goal is only to play good football. I never think of what I want to win, just to have a good time with my football. If you are playing good, enjoyable football then the trophies will take care of themselves.'

In many ways Gullit's debut in the Premier League, against Everton, was the classic Beauty verses the Beast confrontation.

The Dutch dazzler, who personifies total football, against the team with a mean streak and an all-consuming hatred of getting beaten. He didn't flinch the challenge. He was ready to take on all-comers, be they six foot four inch Scotsmen like Duncan Ferguson or five foot seven English midgets. Expectations were running high at Stamford Bridge, which was still undergoing reconstruction work. But the club and their fans were ready to embrace the start of a new and successful era.

CHAPTER FOUR

A New Season, a New Challenge

Remarkable performances, astonishing results, and an inspirational member of the team. Not bad for an opening season. Ruud Gullit inspired a belief that one of the dormant giants of English football is on the march again. Gullit was the catalyst that elevated AC Milan from the obscurity of mid-table in *Serie A* to the world's most formidable club. He has not quite achieved that at Stamford Bridge yet, but he has helped restore Chelsea's pride and renewed the conviction that the club can again challenge for the game's top honours. On a personal level, Gullit attracted the accolades of everyone in the game as well as winning many awards to mark his first season in English football.

On the first day of the 1995/96 season *Football Focus* featured Gullit's debut for Chelsea against the then FA Cup holders, Everton. Gary Lineker picked out Gullit as the potential smash hit of the season.

Lineker told the millions of BBC viewers: 'The arrival of Ruud Gullit is fascinating. He is such a great figure. He will give the game what Klinsmann did, with his personality, big name and also his ability to entrance the media. Unlike Klinsmann, who always said the right things, Gullit is outspoken, and maybe that will be a good thing. The first time I saw him play was back in 1986 when I first joined Barcelona. It might only have been a pre-season game but he got a standing ovation from 100,000 Catalans – even though he missed a penalty!'

Not long after the midday *Football Focus*, the Fulham Road was awash with shiny new blue shirts with 'Gullit' on the back. The street traders were doing brisk business in fanzine style T-shirts. Over Gullit's dreadlocked head were superimposed the words 'Judge Dread: Chelsea's Ruud Boy: Judge, Jury and Executioner'. The match day programme featured the inevitable Gullit feature, but also a little dressing room insight from mickey-taking John Spencer who nicknamed Ruud 'The Big Bird', from *Sesame Street* fame.

Anyone complaining about his massive salary, were put to shame by the amount of cash his mere presence was generating. Gullit-mania was out in force. The sold out signs glistening in the glorious sunshine. His long anticipated Premiership debut had finally arrived, and there was a worldwide TV audience of 250 million. More than 60 countries beamed live pictures with an additional 50 nations screening highlights later in the week. There was a bigger audience for the most anticipated kick-off in League history than even for the Mike Tyson comeback fight! CSI, the company which distributes Premiership games, was inundated with requests. General manager Karl Bistany said: 'You would be hard pressed to find anywhere in the world where you couldn't watch the Premiership. You'll be able to see Premier League matches in places like Vietnam and Cambodia.'

All the off the field hype was not wrecked by on the field anti-climax ... a goalless draw. A flag with Ruud's head superimposed on the body of a Chelsea lion was unfurled and he knew that the fans had taken him to their hearts. He waved back enthusiastically when he was introduced to the crowd. There was a sense of occasion and Ruud Gullit did not disappoint anyone. He enthralled the Chelsea fans and became the most dominant foreign import of the opening Premiership weekend – outshining Dennis Bergkamp and David Ginola. He also spectacularly exploded the myth that he is a geriatric former world number one who has been pensioned off at the Bridge. The Dutchman looked super fit and still a formidable force. One crunching tackle in midfield with the fearsome Joe Parkinson proved that, Gullit showing no fear or hesitation as he lunged into a 50–50 challenge.

Gullit explained to anyone who wanted to listen that it is nonsense to dwell on his five knee operations and suggest he is past his prime. He must have been fed up with the constant probing about his fitness, but he responded politely to all the inquisitive journalists: 'I'm fit enough and after ninety minutes I could still go up front, although the heat made it very difficult for everyone. In the first half I didn't expand a lot of energy. I might have seemed very quiet but I was pacing myself. That enabled me after fifty minutes to do more and by then the opposition were tired. It was all about choosing my right moment, not trying something eight times in the first half and tiring in the second.'

His sheer presence and physical and mental awareness inspired Hoddle to make an amazing assertion: 'It was like an Under-12s team with an 18-year-old playing against them!' He explained: 'A player of this quality makes decisions for other players when the ball is still at his feet. He forces other people to make runs. He has time on the ball even when he is being pressurised.' The longer the game persisted the stronger Gullit became, powering into midfield, dynamic in attack. Unfortunately, as Hoddle put it, 'You can't be in two places at once.'

The *Guardian's* David Lacey put it succinctly: 'To be sure, he began at the back with Sinclair and Johnsen, but he did not so much sweep as supervise … In attack Gullit already looks the part. Chelsea need to discover whether he has been given the correct script.'

Once during that Everton match, Gullit trapped the ball, with the powerful menace of Duncan Ferguson breathing down his neck, when he was on the edge of the Chelsea box and the last line of defence. In one swift movement he gained possession, turned, and launched a sixty yard crossfield pass of sheer perfection. But the most mouth watering episode came eight minutes from the end. He dribbled past three defenders, had a cross knocked out to Mark Hughes whose acrobatic volley was magnificently saved by fellow Welshman Neville Southall in goal.

A crowd of 30,000 was entranced by Gullit's special brand of skill and afterwards even hard-bitten football writers were complimentary about his humble off-the-field approach. He ended his first interview with the media with, 'Have a nice weekend'. When his BBC interview was beamed into the press room he was applauded! 'Different class,' was the comment buzzing around Chelsea's press room. Ruud is such a nice guy, even the most cynical hacks were impressed by his charms.

Before leaving the stadium, Ruud stopped to sign autographs for eager youngsters, ignoring the spitting and snarling of the Everton fans on the other side of the tunnel as they showered their venom at the referee. Their hatred had been whipped up by the injury time yellow card for their hero, Duncan Ferguson. Neil Harman summed it up perfectly in the *Daily Mail*: 'I know who I'm going to prefer watching.'

That night Des Lynam, Alan Hansen and Gary Lineker engaged in an amusing ding-dong as the BBC's *Match of the Day* focused on Gullit. First millions of BBC viewers listened to an enthralling Gullit interview: 'I am really happy here the way we are playing. We controlled most of the game and that is the football Glenn wants us to play. But, of course, it is far from perfect right now, but people have to be patient. I, nor Glenn Hoddle, can transform the way Chelsea play in a couple of weeks.

When I started with Milan we went up and down like a yo-yo right up until December. In my first season we wanted to play 'Total Football' but it took us more than six months to create a good, balanced and strong team.'

Then came the sideshow as Hansen and Lineker analysed Gullit's illuminating performance:

Lynam: 'OK gentlemen, before we discuss how we saw Gullit's debut, first of all is it Hullet, is it Kullet or ...'

Lineker: 'I know how you say it, it's ... Gggggulet!'

Lynam: 'We'll stick with that, then.'

(The ex-England captain jokingly wipes the spit off Alan Hansen's jacket – all three laugh.)

Lineker: 'At least I can say it!'

Lynam: 'No matter how you pronounce his name, the man can still play.'

Hansen: 'It was like watching a Hoddle with pace. He was sensational. He was passing it long, short, into space, into feet. It was all brilliant and he loved to get forward. He made three of Chelsea's best chances. I loved his ability to just hit the ball so long. He does it over sixty yards spot on, so accurate that the defender has no chance. Once he makes a run he keeps going. Gullit played really well. Stamford Bridge supporters already love him.'

Lynam: 'That sweeper's role is very demanding. Can he do that all season?'

Hansen: 'Well, the way he plays it is very demanding. But Gullit surprised me with his fitness level and his pace.'

Lynam: 'Did you spot any negatives?'

Hansen: 'Negatives? What does that mean with this man?'

Lynam: 'Well, you usually come up with one!'

Hansen (laughs): 'He was a bit over elaborate. At one stage he dribbled in his own box. That occasion would give certain managers a heart attack.'

Lineker: 'Well, surely you trust a player like Gullit when he dribbles like that?'

Hansen: 'If you were a manager, would you want Gullit to do that?'

Lineker: 'Shut up! He's such a great player, such a quality player, he will suss it out. He'll soon know which players to give it to and which not.'

Hansen: 'Well, the big test comes when he plays away from home. Maybe he should play the percentages.'

Lineker: 'Would you want Gullit to play in percentages? Of course you don't. We don't have to tell him how to play, he will teach us one or two things.'

Ruud's away debut came three days later at Nottingham Forest and he was relishing the chance to face fellow Dutchman Bryan Roy. Gullit's experience proved vital as a crowd of 27,007 packed into the City ground, swelled by 3,000 travelling Chelsea fans. Roy and Ruud embraced in the pre-match warm up and both conspired to ensure the game ended goalless; one, outstanding in defence, the other missing a glorious chance. Another goalless draw for Chelsea left them in twelfth place after the opening week of the season.

Once again Ruud was all over the field. He engineered chances that Mark Stein twice volleyed over the bar. Although Kevin Campbell, Forest's £2 million signing from Arsenal, struck the bar when it seemed harder to miss in the 17th minute, Chelsea had enough chances to have opened their account for the season. At the final whistle, Gullit strode over to Dmitri Kharine to show his appreciation of the Russian keeper's super show. Also, when Chelsea needed Gullit the most in a second half of intense pressure, he was dominant in the defensive area his critics felt would be his achilles heel.

Forest manager Frank Clark revealed: 'We had worked on preventing Gullit running the game and exploiting the gaps whenever he moved out of the back line. Ruud doesn't exactly hurry back. There was nothing wrong with our plans apart from the fact that we couldn't stick the ball in the net.'

Ruud's passion and commitment was never more in evidence when his frustration spilled over with a verbal rebuke for team-mate Mark Stein when he failed to control one of his perfectly struck passes. But Gullit explained that it was no slight against Stein, more a means of encouragement. He said: 'It is a good thing to get angry, it shows you care and you want to win. If you don't react like that, then apathy can set in. People's heads will go down and down. I like to suddenly wake people up with a bit of shouting. It is meant to encourage and get people going.'

After two successive clean sheets Chelsea suffered their first defeat of the season at Middlesbrough the following week. First Jan-Aage Fjortoft's lightening pass opened up the defence and Nicky Barmby scurried through to set up the opener for Craig Hignett. Then Fjortoft finished Chelsea off with the second. So Boro celebrated the opening of their 30,000, all-seater, £16 million Riverside Stadium by claiming Chelsea's scalp in an emotionally charged game.

Against Boro, Ruud surged forward more and more in the latter stages of the match, while David Lee plugged the gap left behind. Already, it seemed inevitable that Ruud would have to be switched to a more attacking role. At first Hoddle ruled out any immediate change in position, 'He can control things from the back. We have bedded him in that role. We pushed him up front but it was a one-off measure because I would rather be positive if we are losing. I would rather go down 3–0 than not try for a draw.

We'll use him up front as and when required. But we're asking too much of him. The other players are looking to him to set everything up, but they must start to make things happen themselves.'

Ruud was still adamant that his prime role was to dictate the course of events from the back, not the front. 'I cannot afford to go further forward, because the moment I went into midfield, Middlesbrough got the goal. If I play there, it gives us a chance to score but also makes us vulnerable to a counter-attack.'

So Chelsea were the only side in the Premiership yet to score. The all-important goal eventually arrived in their fourth game of the season, a 2–2 draw with Coventry at the Bridge. But an utterly dejected Glenn Hoddle admitted he was totally 'mystified' that Chelsea were still left without a win at the start of Gullit's adventure in English football. Hoddle sat ashen faced as he accused his team of conceding sloppy goals, lacking character and professionalism as they threw away a two-goal lead after a breathtaking start. Gullit's exhilarating angled shot in injury time deserved to be the winner but struck a post.

Dennis Wise scored Chelsea's first goal after Coventry's Brian Burrows had up-ended Gavin Peacock in the penalty box after just six minutes. Then Mark Hughes got off the mark for his new club. He collected his first goal after a moment of stunning quality from Gullit. Positioned on the halfway line on the flank, there seemed no danger until Ruud struck an inch perfect forty yard pass with the outside of his boot that hardly raised an inch off the ground. With stunning accuracy, the ball found Hughes on the edge of the box. The Welshman, using his strength, held off a defender before cracking an angled shot past keeper John Filan.

Ruud celebrated his 33rd birthday on Friday, 1 September. Ten days later he was rejoicing in Chelsea's first win of the season – but he didn't celebrate his first booking! Chelsea beat West Ham 3–1 at Upton Park on Monday, 11 September. It was a night of mixed emotions for Ruud, as he savoured the relief and glory of their first Premiership win of the season, making the first and third goals. Chelsea's third on the stroke of 90 minutes will live on in the memory, with Ruud's extraordinary skills setting up John Spencer's second of the night.

Just a moment before that decisive goal, however, Ruud was shown the yellow card by County Durham referee Robbie Hart for diving. It was a busy night for Hart who filled up his notebook with eight bookings. But when he reached for the yellow card for the final time to raise it in Gullit's face, Ruud looked at him in disgust. Gullit had been heavily tackled by the muscular Danish international centre-half Marc Rieper and tumbled to the ground. It didn't look a dive to this observer but Gullit received his first booking in English football in his fifth appearance in the Premiership.

To be accused of cheating left Ruud furious and bewildered. 'That's the first time anything like that has ever happened to me and I can't say I enjoyed it. I did not dive, I was bundled over. I told the referee that, but he disagreed and booked me. I have to accept that, but I don't like it because that's not my style.'

I reported in the *Daily Mirror* at the time that referee Hart should feel ashamed for booking Gullit for the merest over reaction to a tackle and allowing the Hammers' Julian Dicks to stay on the field. Hart retorted: 'I don't feel ashamed for booking Gullit. He took a dive. He knew what he was doing. I have absolutely no doubt that he dived and deserved a booking. I've no problem with that. He came over to me straight away trying to prove his innocence. He was very polite.'

The match was marred by the Dicks stamping incident with Spencer. Dicks left a gaping gash by Spencer's left ear and the little Scot had to go off for seven minutes for stitches. He returned courageously just before the interval. Hoddle revealed: 'It was a nasty gash, but not a problem. John is a tough Glaswegian and said as he went down the tunnel for the second half, 'Don't take me off'.' He appeared for the second half with his head heavily bandaged.

Gullit unlocked a tight game with a precision manoeuvre in the 31st minute, turning at one end of the pitch, strolling with the ball to the centre circle to deliver a pinpoint pass to the overlapping unmarked Scott Minto. The full-back did justice to the move with a deep cross to the far post where Hughes leapt to head it down and Wise bravely launched himself among the boots to hit it into the corner. Two minutes later Spencer took a short pass from Peacock, to crack a shot out of the reach of Miklosko, the keeper beaten by the sheer pace of the ball.

Four minutes from a thrilling frantic climax, Gullit broke from midfield only to be brought down cynically by Dicks. Knowing Gullit's history of injuries it was a crunching challenge designed to limit his powers. But Chelsea almost punished Dicks. Wise took a quick free-kick and Tim Breaker became the latest yellow card casualty for hacking down Spencer a yard inside the box. Unfortunately for Chelsea, Miklosko dived full stretch to his left to save Wise's penalty.

The Sky live Monday match finished with Gullit presenting the 'Carling Man of the Match' magnum of champagne to John Spencer. Gullit said: 'The man of the match was Mark Hughes, he made it possible to keep the ball and he moved well in the box.' Joking with Spencer he said: 'I hope you get more of these.' Looking at the bandage on his head he added: 'Maybe every time you play with this!'

The home fixture with Southampton brought Gullit's first goal in English football, but the day before was just as eventful. Ruud pranged his brand new car, and then experienced the sheer joy of seeing his two children brought over from Italy. Just a mile from the club's training ground, near Heathrow, he damaged his N-registered Toyota Carina when it skidded on an oily road and went straight into the back of a London taxi. He was only going 10 miles an hour and nobody was hurt. The affable Dutchman said: 'I was lucky. The police saw it and said it was not my fault because the road was oily. When I hit the brakes, the car just slipped. They put sand on the road later, but it was too late for me.'

Chelsea coach Gwyn Williams joked: 'It's the first tackle Ruud has made all season!'

But nothing was going to disturb Ruud as he was so looking forward to the day out with his kids. They were treated to a trip to Oxford Street. Four-year-old Quincy went in search of his favourite Bugs Bunny T-shirt and video. For Ruud it was a shock to the system to discover just how popular he had become in England. He was mobbed and had to pick up his kids and run for it. Normally he will stop to sign autographs, but he would have missed the match the next day if he had signed them all.

Ruud is the most unmistakable figure in soccer since Gazza and this was illustrated when he took his kids to Oxford Street. Ruud said it was a very difficult shopping day: 'I had to keep them in my hands the whole time, so I couldn't stop to sign autographs or to talk. I just had to make my excuses and rush off with the kids. Of course, it is always nice to have such a reception when people come up to you. It shows they appreciate what you are doing. But sometimes people come and invade your privacy and it can be very disturbing when it is denied to you. It is at moments like these you ask for some spare time for yourself. But most of the time I accept it, I'm not going to complain.' It must have been a risk going to such a pubic place, but Ruud did it for Quincy. He explained: 'He is crazy about Bugs Bunny and I promised him a shirt and video.' Ruud escaped to the sanctuary of a park with his camcorder, to record some special moments. Ruud recalled:

'Quincy played with the kids in the park and I recorded it on video camera. It was lovely to see how kids respond to each other. Quincy doesn't speak English, just Italian and a little Dutch, but kids speak one language. You can see that by the way they play together.'

Ruud's first goal in the Premiership, in Chelsea's 3–0 home win over the Saints, was a cracker – an exquisite volley. Such is the quality of Gullit that there was a gaping difference in class between the Dutchman and even the formidable talent of Matthew Le Tissier.

From the moment Gullit, despite his power and size, turned with remarkable delicacy to wrong foot Le Tissier, there was only one player worth watching the whole afternoon. The Southampton star knows a remedy to curtail Gullit's enormous influence – but he failed miserably to implement it. He said: 'The only thing you can do to stop him is to restrict him from having the ball in deep areas so he can't hit his passes. But he pushes into midfield and that is when the damage occurs. In hindsight the only true way to stop him is use a centre-forward who can mark him!' It would be a brave manager who sacrifices his centre-forward simply to stop Gullit.

Southampton's own Dutchman, Ken Monkou, who came on as a substitute against his old club Chelsea, felt that opponents are in awe of Ruud. He argued, 'He is a superstar, and when players look at him they stand back, overawed by his mere presence.'

The hugely approachable Gullit shrugged his shoulders and smiled: 'Opponents overawed by me? I don't know about that, you would have to ask them. I think it is important to be aware of your skills, not to have any doubts about anything, feel good about it and go for it. That's all I do. You never know what to expect, all I can do is express myself at my best.'

Ruud at the age of 21; he doesn't seem to have changed very much – apart from the moustache!

The embryonic Ruud with his mentor manager Johann Cruyff during their days together at Feyenoord.

The man who discovered Ruud – Welshman Barry Hughes, who still resides in Holland. Hughes recommended the young Gullit to Arsenal and Spurs.

His favourite sweeper position is where it all began with Feyenoord in 1982.

Ruud's first big move, to Phillips-owned PSV Eindhoven with fellow new boy Gerald Vanenburg in 1985.

In full flow with PSV, Ruud Gullit was an awesome sight and virtually unstoppable.

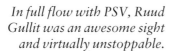

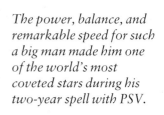

The power, balance, and remarkable speed for such a big man made him one of the world's most coveted stars during his two-year spell with PSV.

Above: Ruud's special way of celebrating PSV's championship success in 1986 – performing his talents as a bass guitarist with a local band while watched by some adoring female fans.

Below: The proud father. Ruud with his first wife, childhood sweetheart Yvonne de Vries, and mother-in-law at the birth of his first baby Felicity (now aged 11) in 1985 in Eindhoven.

Left: Captain of his country in the 1988 European Championships in Germany on his way to the final against Russia, when Ruud turned on the style, scoring a vital goal.

Below: A magical moment for Ruud as he celebrates his country's triumph during the team's lap of honour in Munich.

Above: The Gullit inner-circle is an elite group that includes one of his few confidantes, sports psychologist Ted Troost who has treated and advised him at crucial stages of his career.

Below: Media interviews fail to phase Ruud. Here he is looking perfectly relaxed with Liciana Granello in Sardinia during the 1990 World Cup. Rumours – and don't the Italians love rumours – were that the female reporter became Ruud's 'friend'.

Above: As 1989 European Footballer of the Year, Ruud receives his Adidas award at a glittering ceremony in Paris in January 1990 from Dutch national coach Rinus Michels. He was crowned World Footballer of the Year that same season.

Below: Parading his award alongside the great Dutch striker Marco van Basten, who won the Gold Shoe in the same year. Marco is pictured with his wife and Johann Cruyff.

Above: The 1990 World Cup in Italy. The Dutch team arrive in Sicily to begin their preparations for the opening group games and the security was tight, especially for an instantly recognisable player such as Gullit. Ruud had his own police escort at the airport. Did it bother him? Not a bit. He looked great in those sunglasses.

Below: Gazza on the goal-line with Paul Parker in an anxious moment for England in their World Cup group match against Holland in 1990. Mark Wright and John Barnes are shadowing Frank Rijkaard, Marco van Basten and, of course, the unmistakeable figure of Gullit.

Gullit's first experience of English Cup football was not a good one, to say the least! His cup debut was a goalless draw in the Coca Cola Cup at Stoke on Wednesday, 20th September. Typically, Ruud refused to feel down despite the negative performance from the entire team. It was Ruud's defensive qualities that caught the eye, notably a lunging, perfectly timed tackle inside the penalty area. It is the sort of technique often lacking in an English defender prone to concede a penalty in those circumstances. Ruud showed he can sweat and work with his back-to-the wall as well as show off his attacking prowess. Ruud also sampled another crunching English style tackle from Ray Wallace who nearly cut him off at the knees.

The return leg at Stamford Bridge turned out to be one of the lowest points of Ruud's season. A shock 1–0 defeat – and out of the Cup. Ruud walked off in disgust at the end and it was straight back to the sanctuary of a depressing dressing room. Close behind was Mark Hughes who was the villain of this defeat. A player of his vast experience inexplicably lost possession 15 yards outside of his own penalty area in a challenge from the diminutive Ray Wallace, going down looking for a foul that was never given. Canadian international Paul Peschisolido coolly eluded Frank Sinclair and clipped his shot calmly over Kharine. Hoddle was furious with the error and highly critical of Hughes' mistake, describing it as 'a cardinal sin'. This was by far their worst performance since the arrival of Gullit and Hughes. All the deficiencies in Hoddle's team were cruelly exposed by a vibrant Stoke side determined to enjoy their Cup exploits and ignoring their lowly 20th position in Division One. Lou Macari's team might have arrived just 40 minutes before the kick off, but they made Chelsea seem late to every ball.

With defeat staring his side in the face, Gullit moved into a permanent midfield position to try to salvage Chelsea's Wembley

CHAPTER FIVE

Dreaming of Total Football

Gullit's level of consistency in the 1995/96 season was an object lesson for everyone in the game. On numerous occasions, as sweeper, or in midfield, or on the right wing, or in attack, he reached heights of near perfection. He achieved more ten out of ten performances than one would have considered humanly possible. And he hardly ever fell below nine or eight out of ten!

Consistency is only a tiny part of the story. It was sheer pleasure to chart his first season in the Premiership, a delight to watch his multitude of techniques, to simply marvel at his presence. Even at his age, he was still one of the world's most entertaining talents. Glenn Hoddle had a panache for the 60 yard pass. I enjoyed watching that skill for a decade at Spurs, but even Hoddle's mastery of this technique was overshadowed by Gullit. Hoddle would strike those wondrous long range passes with around 50 per cent accuracy, and it seemed no-one in English football could do it better. Then, along came this guy with something like an incredible 95 per cent accuracy.

As the season progressed Ruud accepted a midfield role, abandoning his preference as sweeper. Peter Shreeves explained the switch: 'We loved him as sweeper, but when he came out with the ball I suppose you'd say he left a few gaps which we weren't too happy with. What teams were doing was pushing one player up to stop him coming out. It was a learning process for all of us.' Seven goals conceded in two matches in October, albeit against Manchester United and Blackburn Rovers, brought matters to a head. Chelsea reverted, momentarily, to a flat back four but reintroduced the system with David Lee as sweeper – and with considerable success – while Gullit was out for seven weeks with a calf injury. When he returned, Chelsea had to play him elsewhere, in an attacking role in midfield, and discovered to their delight that he was still capable of being just as much of a threat as he was at the height of his powers in *Serie A*.

A big breakthrough for Hoddle's game plan falling into place was the £2.3 million arrival of Dan Petrescu. The Romanian World Cup star, signed from Sheffield Wednesday, said: 'I want to play for a club with ambition and ability. Having played against Ruud Gullit while we were in Italy, I know what he's all about. I want to move to London and play with him at Chelsea.' Capped more than 50 times for his country, Petrescu got his wish. At Steau Bucharest he won the Romanian championship four times and reached the European Cup Final – where AC Milan won 4–0 with Ruud scoring twice. Petrescu's arrival marked the end of a determined campaign by Hoddle, who had been tracking the defender for seven months.

On the eve of Chelsea's match against Manchester United in October 1995, Mark Hughes compared his old and new club. Hughes said: 'Glenn Hoddle has a vision of what must be done here. I know there have been many false dawns for Chelsea in the past, but now you sense we are on the brink of a major break-through. There is real quality here, especially in the form of Ruud Gullit. People use the phrase world-class too cheaply in football. In all my time in the game, I might have played alongside three or four genuine world-class players. I'd put Eric Cantona and Bryan

Robson in that category. Gullit is up there with the very best.'

Against Manchester United, Gullit played in defence, then midfield and in attack. Pity he couldn't play in all three at the same time! Here was the evidence, if it were ever really needed, that Gullit was in urgent need of more quality players on the same wavelength, as Chelsea were put in their place with a 4–1 defeat. While Scholes had Chelsea on their knees with two goals inside nine minutes the eldest of the Ferguson babes, Ryan Giggs, scored a wonder goal ten minutes from the end to nullify any thought of a Chelsea revival when Hughes scored against his old club.

Gullit was Chelsea's only hope of salvation. His long-range passing was again so accurate it was the one route for Chelsea's attack. Manchester United captain Steve Bruce observed: 'He's a class player, so comfortable in possession it's a joy to watch him at times.'

Gullit started the match in defence but by the end was leading the attack. Hoddle explained: 'We had to take the risk, it was time to gamble when we were 2–0 down at home. It's not my way to shut up shop and ride out the storm. I want to try and win matches. He moved into midfield in the second half, we were chasing the game, and that's not always ideal because we have to reshape the side.'

Frank Sinclair's red card for a wild challenge on United substitute Brian McClair just about summed up Chelsea's humiliating afternoon. But Ruud did not feel that United were three goals better than Chelsea. 'No, I don't think so. At 2–1 we had some chance to go 2–2 and we had to take a risk.' There was a lengthy de-briefing from Hoddle. 'Yeh, that's normal,' said Gullit.

Ruud performed his usual round of TV interviews, as his two girls, Felicity and Sharmayne, who were over with their grandma from Italy, played happily around the pitch, taking pictures of their dad as he posed with the new stand in the background.

Clearly, he was as happy to see them as they were delighted to be with their father. The early night air was punctuated with cries of laughter and Ruud speaking his native tongue with his two 'Italian daughters'.

Body language can say more than a thousand diplomatic words. For much of the 3–0 defeat at Blackburn that followed the setback against Manchester United, the big man had been trying to keep his finger in the leaking dyke of a defence before moving into midfield. At the end, shoulders slumped and head shaking, Gullit could not get off Ewood Park quick enough. For an hour he sat in the dressing room as he tried to face the harsh realities of attempting to find the way forward.

When he moved into midfield for the last half hour it was pure poetry. But Chelsea were still a shambles at the back. Gullit emerged to give his views: 'Blackburn played well, but you need that luck. Their first goal deflected off me and it sent Dmitri Kharine the wrong way. The second goal showed Alan Shearer's great skill. He always waits for the right moment.'

It was only when Gullit went into the heart of the action that Chelsea looked at all threatening. He set up chances that Mark Stein should have converted. Hoddle was so distraught that he held an hour long inquest in the dressing rooms. Two thrashings in a week was hard to take.

The inevitable occurred on Saturday, 4 November in the goalless draw with Sheffield Wednesday at the Bridge ... Ruud played in midfield for the first time. And, he produced a superb performance, until he suffered a calf injury. But it was a bad result, and a ridiculous booking for mischievously pretending not to give the ball back for a Wednesday free-kick. Referee Paul Danson showed him the yellow card. Hoddle said: 'This was the first time Ruud has played in an out-and-out midfield position for us, but ideally I want to play him at the back even though he'll always get into midfield positions during games. Today it was a question of shaping the team around the personnel available.'

Hoddle made four changes, abandoning the sweeper system. Sadly, Gullit's colleagues once again failed to read his quick-thinking mind and they either stumbled or were blocked by the brilliance of Wednesday keeper Kevin Pressman. Dan Petrescu was paraded before the game, and his control and class was clearly needed, particularly by Gullit. Ruud finally left the field with an injured calf muscle and with him went any semblance of vision. Most of the time, Gullit's frustration was evident.

The signing of full-back Terry Phelan from Manchester City was overshadowed by board room squabbling between chairman Ken Bates and co-director Matthew Harding. But Ruud was sure the arguments in the board room were not seeping through to the players. He said: 'No, the behind-the-scenes business is miles away from me and the players. The playing staff don't know what goes on in the boardroom on a day-to-day basis, so it doesn't really affect us. I hope for the Chelsea fans and the team that they sort out the problem quickly.'

Ruud missed his first match of the season as Chelsea lost 1–0 at Elland Road on Saturday, 18th November. The London side crashed to a controversial Tony Yeboah goal. It came ten minutes from the end when Chelsea claimed that Kharine was obstructed by the lanky Brian Deane, the ball spilling to the grateful Yeboah.

It may have been the bottom club, but it was vital to have beaten Bolton 3–2 at the Bridge the following week to end the slump. It was a match the Chelsea manager had to win. And, by the way Hoddle leapt in the air and hugged his assistant Peter Shreeves at the sight of Eddie Newton's last gasp winner, you would think he was celebrating an FA Cup triumph at Wembley. Hoddle's team ended a disastrous slump that had coincided with a bitter board room battle.

Chelsea finally began to put an impressive run of results together despite the absence of Gullit, and with a new youthful defensive formation. David Lee had taken over in the sweeper role, and young Michael Duberry was making a remarkable impact. Andy Myers completed the new three-at-the-back line-up. Ruud missed the next game, but even without his influence, the team claimed a notable result at Old Trafford, drawing 1–1 with United.

Next came the shock Premiership win over Newcastle at the Bridge. Dan Petrescu grabbed the only goal, just before half-time, when a Dennis Wise free-kick was knocked out to him. Newcastle goalkeeper Pavel Srnicek had only come on seconds before for the injured Shaka Hislop. At the end of the match, Wise waved in triumph at Ken Bates and Matthew Harding in the directors box. Meanwhile, Kevin Keegan waved goodbye to another disappointing journey to London. Keegan, tasted defeat for only the second time in the season, and he didn't like it. He said: 'The first half was a joke, too many of my players didn't play well. They didn't look like they had the appetite for it. They took half a day off, wouldn't we all like half a day off.'

There was more good news with a vast improvement in Ruud's recovery rate. Physio Mike Banks said: 'Ruud tore his calf muscle against Sheffield Wednesday and you're always out four weeks minimum with an injury like that. He's just been through his fifth week but is not quite ready. We have been holding him back a little in the sense of not rushing him because it's easy to tear again and you can be out another four or five weeks.'

In front of just 200 odd fans on Kingstonian's ground at Kingston on Thames, Ruud made his long awaited comeback on Monday, 18th December. Again, a far cry from the San Siro, but it was a match that Ruud relished, even though it was the first reserve game of his illustrious career. He played 80 minutes at a comfortable pace as Chelsea reserves beat Southampton 2–1. Ruud laid on the opening goal in the 41st minute, keeper Bruce Grobbelaar failing to hold his cross for Paul Furlong to poke into an empty net. He said: 'It was hard work after six weeks out and it hurt. I needed a massage afterwards. Now I will do some more work but I need a few more games to get my fitness back. I don't know if I will be ready for the holiday games. That could depend on what the gaffer wants. I'm naturally fit because I look after myself.'

Ruud made his Premiership comeback at Maine Road on Saturday 23rd December. He was not even expected to feature in this game after only a week back in training and a single reserve team outing. Now Gullit was a fully fledged midfield player.

He showed glimpses of his old class before setting up the winning goal for Gavin Peacock. Gullit dispossessed young left-back Rae Ingram, and then with a surprising sudden surge of power, cut in to slide the ball on to Peacock's toe for a simple tap-in. Peacock had also been a long-term injury victim and would not have played but for a chest infection that struck down Dennis Wise on the morning of the match. In the event, Hoddle's double gamble on the maker and scorer paid off handsomely.

The same could not be said of all the effort that week – including talking to the European Court of Justice – that Manchester City had put into winning the right to play an extra foreigner during the week. Starting with two Germans, Eike Immel and Uwe Rosler, plus the Georgian Georgi Kinkladze on the field, they were full of early menace with Rosler and Gerry Creaney missing excellent chances in the first six minutes.

Chelsea gradually asserted themselves after that shaky beginning and made and missed the best of the subsequent chances, with John Spencer – from a superb Gullit pass – Petrescu and Hughes the most guilty men. But this was Chelsea at their most expressive in terms of passing. At times it was a joy to watch. Chelsea were moving the ball around with growing confidence. Their Gullit-inspired winner was the mark of a side which had turned around both their season and this particular contest.

Hoddle said the decision to bring back Gullit early had paid off: 'The big man has only trained for a few days and played one reserve game, so putting him in was a risk. But this pitch is big and I didn't think anyone could get near him. With him in the side, I always believe our performance goes up a couple of notches and that's how it looked against City. Ruud is naturally fit, but whether he plays in all the Christmas games is another matter. While it was great to have Gullit back, this wasn't just a one-man show.'

Of course, not all of Chelsea's matches were an exhibition of the 'Beautiful Game'. One example was the clash with Everton at Goodison Park on 13 January. The game ended 1–1 but all the attention centred on Hughes' dismissal. He was shown the red card by referee Robbie Hart for allegedly 'stamping' on David Unsworth. That gave him a three-match ban. And he missed two more games because he had earlier picked up a yellow card for 'persistent misconduct' which took him beyond the 31-point disciplinary threshold.

After a subdued first half, Gullit was much more influential after the break, despite being the victim of a crude late lunge from Craig Short which amazingly escaped punishment from the baffling Hart. Yet, all it provoked was the moronic booing of the classy Gullit. Neil Bramwell, in the *Independent* wrote: 'There is a body of thought that, while the Premiership is open house for foreign stars, not enough is done to pamper the likes of Ruud Gullit. David Ginola is accustomed to his every touch being booed, every trick demolished by a scything pair of size 12s and every stray elbow subjected to intense scrutiny. Gullit, the only import who can touch the Newcastle player for flair, has so far only suffered the physical rigours of English football. There are signs, though, that other trials are just around the corner. The Goodison crowd took exception to a couple of theatricals straight from the Ginola textbook. There were also indications of a growing tetchiness in his relations with colleagues. Gullit is not slow to show displeasure when his team-mates do not meet his own standards. And more than one Chelsea player felt the need to vent their feelings when Gullit was slow to fulfil the defensive obligations of his roaming role.'

A more pleasing performance was against Nottingham Forest at Stamford Bridge. Ruud's Dutch friend Bryan Roy made the pertinent observation of the improvement in the Chelsea team with a new look defence and Gullit in midfield. He said: 'I felt Ruud was being wasted as a sweeper but now he has been moved into a more advanced position, where he is going to be dangerous. The further forward he plays, the more of a threat Ruud becomes. I've seen some of the games he has played in midfield and he's made a big difference. I would play him as a striker and then Chelsea would get 15 goals out of him at least. In his last season with Sampdoria he was superb as a striker. He's the most devastating in the world in that position – I would place him alongside Cruyff and Van Basten.'

Chelsea beat Forest 1–0 as Hoddle's master plan was beginning to take shape – and get noticed. The acquisition of 'wing-backs' Terry Phelan and Dan Petrescu were vital cogs in the Hoddle machinery while Michael Duberry was developing quickly into the discovery of the season, enabling Gullit to roam with greater menace in midfield. England left-back Stuart Pearce observed a vast improvement in the side Forest had played in the opening week of the season. 'They have changed both their full-backs and brought in two who enjoy going forward. Glenn has shaped the team how he wants it to play. They knock it about around midfield with Gullit and Wise orchestrating it and it's very difficult to do anything about it when they've got the ball.'

It had taken Hoddle two and a half years to come close to the perfection he was seeking in his particular style of play. He confessed after the win over Forest: 'This is the most enjoyable time for me since I came to the club, and it is very important to me that we are able to play this way. The system means you have to have good attacking full-backs and I've been looking and looking. They are the key to the whole situation.' The final piece of the jigsaw for Hoddle was to turn the chances into goals.

John Spencer swept in a Petrescu cross, but Chelsea hardly ever looked likely to find the comfort of a second goal. Yet, Hoddle's team were showing a Continental sophistication. Hoddle is one of the few managers convinced that English players are capable of intricate-possession football. He observed: 'It's the best run of matches since I've been in charge in terms of consistency. Even when we reached the FA Cup Final two seasons ago and the semi-final of the European Cup Winners' Cup last season we were not playing as well as this. I've sat on the bench watching the lads play – I've been entertained. As well as wearing your professional hat in wanting and needing to win matches, I've enjoyed the job because we've taken it up a couple of cogs. And that's what I've always wanted to do. I felt we needed to get the right people. We're getting there. Some of our football has been as good as any in the country. Looking at us now, people can no longer say we are a one, two or even three-man team. A lot of people said we would really struggle when Ruud Gullit was injured in November, but in fact we have lost only one of our last 13 games. It's wonderful to have a player of Ruud's quality back with us now, but we've proved we can cope without him.'

Sky TV set out to find out how good Gullit is by setting up their computer to analyse his every move in their Sunday soccer special on 4th February featuring Chelsea against Middlesbrough. They certainly picked the right match … Chelsea won 5–0!

Gullit's statistics were illuminating:

48 passes

(37 completed)

3 key passes (all led to goals)

2 tackles

(1 won)

Dennis Wise, who was suspended for the match, was one of Sky's 'experts'. He enthused: 'Ruud is capable of anything. He does everything simple – except those 50 yard passes!'

A euphoric Hoddle celebrated Chelsea's biggest league win in the top flight for thirty-two years by declaring: 'We were fantastic. That's the best we've played in the two-and-a-half years I've been at the club. Everything we've been working at for the last two years is falling into place.'

Hoddle's team was upwardly mobile, but by comparison Bryan Robson's side were sinking like a stone in the Premiership. The Chelsea fans mockingly chanted 'Robson for England' as his team were totally outclassed by a style of football more suited to the international stage than perhaps anything else in the English game. Hoddle had successful re-educated the Chelsea fans with more than just 'Total Football' with the exquisite Gullit in the side, but with 'Pure Continental'. Three at the back, two wing-backs and possession football, a majestic fluency and on this occasion a striking potency.

Shorn of the Brazilian blend provided by Juninho, Boro could hardly get the ball away from a Chelsea team indoctrinated in the sophisticated art of passing the ball from one player to another that used to be the hallmark of Hoddle as a player. Of course, Hoddle could not achieve this continental approach without the influence of Gullit, Romanian Dan Petrescu, Republic of Ireland international Terry Phelan and Scot John Spencer.

Without the suspended Mark Hughes and Dennis Wise, Gavin Peacock was more than an able stand-in and he plundered the first hat-trick for Chelsea in six years. Chelsea climbed above Arsenal into eighth place with a performance that had Hoddle drooling with delight. Hoddle had been entertained in recent weeks, sitting on the bench, watching his beliefs taking shape before his very eyes. But this was sheer ecstasy.

If there was an award to a player for 'pass of the season', Gullit would be one of the favourites. He hit one of his special 50 yarders in the 52nd minute that landed inch perfect at the feet of Petrescu, whose chip was finished off by Paul Furlong. The chant was 'Ruudi, Ruudi' in appreciation of a masterly pass by the Dutchman. That destroyed Boro who had, no doubt, been told by Robson at half-time to go out and play for their pride and try to redeem themselves after conceding three goals in the first half. The first goal came after 29 minutes when David Lee's near post corner was knocked out only as far as Peacock lurking just inside the box. Peacock's sideways shot bounced in the corner with Gullit standing in an offside position obscuring keeper Gary Walsh's vision, but referee Keith Cooper was lenient. That was clearly the turning point as Boro never recovered.

Just two minutes later Petrescu searched out Spencer whose angled shot found the corner. That goal was typical of Chelsea's free movement and passing game and the third was inevitable when Spencer sent Gullit galloping through. Gullit looked assured of grabbing a goal for himself but unselfishly squared the ball past Walsh for Peacock to slide into an unguarded goal. The fourth goal was a delight and Spencer decided that anything Gullit could do, he could try as well, with a devastating long range pass for Peacock in the 55th minute to complete the first Chelsea hat-trick since Kerry Dixon in 1990. Boro substitute Paul Wilkinson struck the post in the last minute with a 20 yard shot and keeper Kevin Hitchcock produced one excellent save from Fjortoft just before half-time. But the 21,060 crowd were treated to an exhibition of the sort of football that made the FA sit up and take notice of Hoddle's credentials to become England coach.

Gullit was simply breathtaking, but Hoddle stressed: 'One man can't do it on his own. Obviously Ruud is a great player and he's enjoying the way we are playing, but it is because the others are slotting in so well around him. I'm very pleased with the way things are coming together. We're achieving good football and good results and I've always believed this is the correct way to play – pass and move just like Liverpool and Manchester United have done over the years. We've been close to playing like that a few times and now we are just three points off fourth place.'

Hoddle's happiness should have been complete, but he was surprised that the fans did not appear to be getting behind him and the team. 'I was disappointed with the support. They could have got behind us more. They were seeing some sensational football out there but at times it went a bit quiet. They've had a hard time here for a long time and they should have been taking the roof off over that performance. We probably won't play as well as that again all season and they should have done it. The passing and movement was everything I have been dreaming of. I always knew it could be done – it was a superb performance, probably the best by a Chelsea team for a very long time. We've won nothing yet, although we are achieving something with the way we are playing and hopefully we can get better and better. Now we've got to go on and win something. We've got to believe in ourselves, continue to play in this way and not get too big-headed about everything. But I think good times could be ahead.'

When Chelsea faced Southampton at the Dell on 24 February,

there was close attention paid to the meeting of two of the most skilful players in the Premiership – Gullit and Matthew Le Tissier. Hoddle's message to Le Tissier in his desire to play for England was to watch and learn from Ruud. He explained: 'Gullit shows the difference there is between a good player and a great one. He is an example to everyone. Matt is a very talented player but he has trouble finding his best form every week. He should watch Ruud in action and see how he influences the whole team. Matt gets a hard time because he is expected to do something wonderful whenever he gets the ball. But you can't do that, although it gets to the stage when you feel under pressure to try and make it happen. The crowd and the critics always want you to do it, so when it doesn't come off, you get down and it's hard to pull yourself out of the slump. That's where Ruud is so impressive. He can make simple passes and really dictate the play, making others perform to the best of their ability, even when he's not at his own peak. Mattie simply needs to get in the game, like Ruud. Then he'll see that the spectacular stuff will come along with a bit of hard work.'

The match at the Dell went precisely to Glenn's script with Ruud scoring a stunning goal. Mark Hughes, in his first game back after a five-match ban, was superb up front, taking terrible stick from the Southampton defence yet still setting up two magnificent goals. Gullit's pass that set up Wise's first half penalty was as good as you'll see anywhere, and it delighted Ruud as much as his outstanding goal. He said: 'That pass of mine pleased me more than my goal because it was at a delicate stage for us.'

Ruud's goal was featured on *Match of the Day* with Trevor Brooking describing him as 'a unique talent.' Ruud said: 'I have a new role from my AC Milan days and I am enjoying it. In my new role it is difficult to score goals. I am the one who gets the ball and has to do something with it. But I suppose it was an important goal and I did have to run 70 yards to score it. If you like football, that goal was perfect. It may look easy, but it is not done so easily.'

Hoddle joked: 'He kept his AC Milan head on as a striker.' He explained: 'Ruud was as cool as a cucumber. From my angle, I thought the ball was going over the bar but then it just dipped in. Then again, from my angle I had a good view of the linesman's boots!'

Ruud's winning goal was an object lesson to Le Tissier ... even the most gifted players still have to sweat. 'Ruud was magnificent as usual but everyone talks about him so much that they overlook Hughes' contribution,' Wise said. 'He's come straight back after a month off and done everything we wanted. He held the ball up and he was just fantastic.'

Wise's first goal, curled in from 20 yards after Tommy Widdrington had fired Saints into an early lead, was just the prelude. Le Tissier also came close after setting up Neil Shipperley for the Saints' second but he never even challenged Gullit for the man-of-the-match award. In terms of natural ability, there's probably not a lot to choose between the two. But when it comes to application, it's no contest. Gullit accelerated from deep inside his own half to exchange passes with Hughes before sending an exquisite chip over Beasant for the winning goal.

Ruud's view of Le Tissier: 'He is a great player and he almost scored a late goal for them. It was difficult for him today, they gave him every ball and he has to look for the right path. It can't be easy. But without hard work you will achieve nothing. It starts when you're at home. You must eat well, go to bed early, don't drink and don't smoke much. That's how I was raised and I believe that if you're going to be the best you have to show it and make sure others get better from playing with you. You have to work harder than the rest because that's what's expected of you. If you set a good example, then they do the same thing. You work on your tackling and your all-round game as much as you do on free-kicks and ball control.'

Dave Merrington knew it was a 'no contest' between Le Tiss and Ruud. 'No comment,' was the Saints manager's response to his star players contribution. As for Gullit, he enthused: 'I do admire Gullit. His talent is God-given – and how he uses it. If any player wants to watch and learn about technique and approach, then Gullit is the one to go and see. He is so uncomplicated, there is so much we can learn from him. That is the way the game should be played. I take one look at Gullit and I can see that he made all the difference.'

February 1995 was an tremendous month for Ruud and he was awarded the *Evening Standard* Player of the Month. Columnist Trevor Brooking enthused about the classy foreign imports to the Premiership. He wrote: 'This month I saw Eric Cantona and Ruud Gullit enthral supporters with two outstanding individual displays which were a marvellous mixture of skill, flair and arrogance. It must be a wonderful learning experience for the younger players at both Manchester United and Chelsea. But their presence also gives young fans the opportunity to witness exceptional skills first hand.' Brooking marvelled at Cantona's skills and restraint on his return to Selhurst Park with two goals against Wimbledon. But he went on: 'If anything, Gullit's display against Middlesbrough was even more awesome. Since moving forward into midfield he has displayed the complete range of footballing skills. He was like a great conductor as he strutted around the pitch orchestrating a delightful series of intricate passing moves which bemused and destroyed the opposition. It was a fitting reward for manager Glenn Hoddle after 30 months in charge at Stamford Bridge, and suddenly the fruits are starting to spring forth after all the hard work carried out on the training ground. Even the manager himself might have been hard pushed to match some of Gullit's long, raking cross-field passes which dropped tantalisingly into the stride of the grateful recipient.'

Chelsea may have been producing beautiful football and entertaining the fans but were they going to win honours? Hoddle said at the beginning of the season that Chelsea's best chance for success was in one of the Cups. In his first year at Stamford Bridge, Hoddle had taken his side to the FA Cup Final – this year he tried to repeat that and give Ruud Gullit the opportunity to display his class at Wembley.

CHAPTER SIX

Cup Battles

There are games that will live forever in the memory. Not just for Chelsea fans, but Ruud Gullit himself. He thought he had seen it all, and done it all, in his majestic career. But then again the fervour of the FA Cup has to be experienced first hand.

The recuperating Ruud watched Chelsea open their FA Cup campaign at the Bridge on Sunday, 7 January against Kevin Keegan's Newcastle United. After 35 minutes Chelsea took the lead when Wise manoeuvred out of a tight corner with an excellent pass to the ever overlapping full-back Phelan. His cross to the far post was met by Mark Hughes whose header marked his return from suspension with a goal that looked like knocking Newcastle out of the Cup. Hughes also had a couple more chances but wasted his angled shots, while Newcastle struggled to create genuine openings.

But there was to be a shock ending in store for Chelsea with Ruud perched high in the directors' box. Three minutes into injury time Les Ferdinand snatched victory from Chelsea, scoring with his one and only chance when Kharine lost out in a game of Russian roulette in the 93rd minute of a pulsating tie. Ferdinand's goal rescued Newcastle's dream of a League and Cup double. Kharine took his time over a goal kick only to scoop his clearance half his normal distance, and Philippe Albert astutely headed into the stride of Ferdinand. A frantic Kharine raced off his line but Ferdinand was first to the ball slipping it through the Russian keeper's legs.

With Chelsea under siege, near the end of the game, Hoddle was on his feet furiously pointing at his watch and shouting at referee Stephen Lodge. After the match, Hoddle made his way into the referee's dressing-room for a confrontation over the 'extra' six minutes added to normal time. Hoddle was furious Newcastle had equalised in the 93rd minute and Lodge had allowed play to go on for another three minutes. Hoddle said calmly: 'Am I angry? Am I upset? Let's say I'm putting a brave face on it. We have a stop watch on every game we play. When I confronted the ref he never really said why he added on so much time. He said it was four minutes. We thought it was six. It felt more like an hour.'

Hoddle went on: 'When I went to see him, I didn't shout or yell, just calmly asked him for an explanation. I wanted to know if his watch had stopped. But that's it. There's nothing we can do about it. We got punished for a mistake when I felt we deserved to win. The boys are sitting in the dressing room distraught. It was a killer punch so late in the game. Dmitri Kharine is a professional. And you always know when you've made a mistake. You can't blame him. We had the chances to make it 2–0, and then his mistake wouldn't have mattered. It's something that you have to take.'

Keegan conceded: 'We thought we were out of it. Am I relieved? Obviously. But we never stopped believing. When Philippe Albert missed in the final seconds, I thought that was the last throw of the dice for us. We played better in the second half, it was impossible not to. Before that we lacked passion, and you have to have that in the Cup, League and in life. We never come down here and seem to do ourselves justice but, after the interval, we just threw caution to the winds. In the end, we were a little bit lucky to get out of it.'

Referee Stephen Lodge insisted that Hoddle got it wrong in his timing. He said: 'I don't care if Chelsea had a man in the dug-out timing the game. The person with sole responsibility for ensuring the full 90 minutes were played is me – and, no, my watch does not need repairing. Hoddle came to see me in my room after the game and said: 'I'm not blaming you for the fact that our keeper made a cock-up.' I told him that I stopped the clock for all the stoppages, not just the three occasions in the second half when the stretchers came on. I was surprised and disappointed to read his claim that he did not get a proper response out of me. He came to see me in a proper and courteous manner – and I gave him a courteous explanation.'

Gullit was back in the Chelsea side for the replay at St James' Park. It turned out to be an enthralling cut and thrust match, packed with incident, that will long be remembered by the near 37,000 crowd privileged to be present. Les Ferdinand had rescued his side at Stamford Bridge and the England striker signalled his intent in the replay when he crashed a tremendous 25 yard drive against the foot of the post to set a thrilling night in motion. Ginola was looking dangerous on the left, and then Ferdinand created the opening goal. David Lee hauled him down just outside the area, and with the home fans baying for his blood, referee Stephen Lodge awarded a free-kick. Albert's effort took a fierce deflection off Wise to send Newcastle into the lead four minutes before the break. Chances were missed at either end and Kevin Hitchcock pulled off a wonderful one-handed save from Paul Kitson before the match exploded on the hour mark.

Newcastle centre-back Darren Peacock, who had been booked in the first half, brought down Spencer and was shown the red card. Wise scored the resultant penalty to level. But within three minutes, Lodge, who had a poor match, ruled that Duberry had fouled Kitson, and awarded another penalty. Beardsley, celebrating his 35th birthday the next day, gleefully smashed it home, and Newcastle looked to be on their way. But Chelsea never panicked and kept playing their neat passing game. They threw men forward, pushing Gullit up from midfield to a centre-forward's role, and they slowly turned the screw. Srnicek made a string of vital stops from Gullit, Spencer and Lee, but in the dying seconds Chelsea's bold plan sensationally paid off.

From yet another cross, Gullit scored in the 89th minute to force the match into extra time. It was only Gullit's second goal in English soccer, and no matter how many he may go on to score, he will never forget the stunning leveller which kept Chelsea in the Cup. John Spencer's cross curled over from the left and the Dutchman bravely charged in to hook the ball over keeper Pavel Srnicek. It took all of Ruud's athleticism to perform the simple touch for such a vital goal. Gullit was hugged by his ecstatic team-mates as they all appreciated the importance of the goal.

After no further goals in extra-time the game went to a penalty shoot-out, which could not have been more dramatic. Newcastle skipper Peter Beardsley, who scored from the spot in normal time, crashed the first effort against the bar. Cool Chelsea centre-back David Lee whacked his straight down the middle. 1–0 to Chelsea. Newcastle's Steve Watson, a scorer of three crucial winners for his team that season, couldn't do it again as his low shot was saved by keeper Kevin Hitchcock. Captain Dennis Wise, a strong contender for Man of the Match, smacked his effort high into the top right hand corner. 2–0 to Chelsea. John Beresford scored Newcastle's first with a low drive into the left hand side.

Chelsea substitute Gavin Peacock then converted low against his old club to make the score 3–1 to Chelsea. The vastly experienced Belgian international, Philippe Albert responded with another low drive to make it 3–2. But Eddie Newton sent Chelsea supporters delirious with another low hard penalty to take Chelsea through to a fourth round derby at Queens Park Rangers.

Ruud was so emotional, he threw his shirt into the throng of Chelsea fans, so too did Wise. Ruud spoke at greater length before stepping aboard the Chelsea team bus. He revealed why he missed the dramatic shoot-out – he hates penalties. He admitted: 'I don't like the shoot-out because it's so cruel. If you look back through my career, you'll find I never took a penalty. Everybody has to know his own limits. I prefer to score goals from open play.' That prompted a typical Ruud roar of laughter. He added: 'It's nothing to do with tension. We had players who can kick it very well, so why should I be like "I'm a big shot, I should do it"?'

The accolades for the team performance and Gullit's contribution came first from manager Glenn Hoddle. He said: 'Ruud was superb for us. For the first time this week he has been injury free and it showed.' But Hoddle saluted all his heroes. 'You feel that after two titanic battles like that we should jump to the semi-finals.'

The result at St James' was ironic for one particular Newcastle player – Peter Beardsley. Before the season started, the England and Newcastle forward had cast grave doubts about Chelsea's credentials to succeed despite Gullit's presence. Beardsley questioned Gullit's role as a sweeper in a *Sunday Mirror* article. The headline was: 'England star's shock verdict will really stick in the Gullit.' It must have stuck in Beardsley's Gullet!

Beardsley suggested: 'I am not sure Gullit is at a big enough club or a good enough team to be a big hit. I think Gullit would be … if Chelsea were able to play a way that suited him, because he's a great player and that will never change. But Chelsea aren't good enough to play the way his former clubs Sampdoria and AC Milan have in Italy. Obviously the Italians are quality and I'm not saying that Chelsea are a bad team – but I'm not sure they are good enough to let him play the same free role he enjoyed at Sampdoria, I just don't think they are good enough. Gullit is a great player but it seems strange that he's playing for Chelsea in a sweeper's role. I'm sure he will play well there but I'm not sure Chelsea are strong enough around him to protect him. He'll certainly do his thing – but I'm not sure about the rest of them being strong enough to live with him.' Well, to be fair to Beardsley, at least he did get it right about Gullit's role as a sweeper, but he clearly didn't envisage the shrewd switch by Hoddle to play him in midfield, where he was so effective in the Cup tie at Newcastle.

Remarkably, Ruud had a premonition that Chelsea would come through at Newcastle. The day before he was brimming full of confidence even though the rest of the country expected Newcastle to knock out Chelsea. Ruud said: 'There is a tremendous spirit in the team now and we think we can win. Newcastle know we are a good side after we outplayed them twice at home.' Both times without Gullit in the team!

Chelsea faced Queens Park Rangers in the fourth round on Monday, 29th January. The hero of the night was Gullit again, who had fallen in love with this competition. But ultimately the tie hinged on yet another penalty. Young Bradley Allen cracked his 70th minute penalty a yard wide of the right hand upright after Kevin Hitchcock blundered into Mark Hateley.

Hoddle handed the captain's armband to Gullit, who was given a new role in the centre of midfield in the absence of first choice skipper Dennis Wise, starting a two-match ban. With Mark Hughes banished for five matches, a greater responsibility than ever before fell on those huge shoulders. Not only did he produce a typically mesmeric performance, he was cajoling his team-mates and battling it out with the best in the tackle. Wilkins' team led a late revival, but it was the wise old head of Gullit who tried to restore the possession football that had threatened to swamp Rangers earlier in the match.

There was more than a touch of fortune when Chelsea went ahead in the 19th minute. Gullit started a move that involved Dan Petrescu and John Spencer with Gavin Peacock's shot, blocked by Andy Impey, wickedly looping over the head of Juregen Sommer.

The Rangers' fans quickly became disenchanted as Chelsea kept the ball for such long periods, but Nigel Quashie hauled Rangers back into contention with a sweetly struck half volley to the far top corner after Ian Holloway's corner was knocked out to him by Duberry. It launched a Rangers comeback that might have forced a replay but for Allen's penalty blunder. But when Chelsea where being steamrolled out of their silky smooth stride, Gullit could be relied upon to produce something special. With his back to goal, just inside QPR territory, he flicked the ball up and released it over his shoulder inch perfect, cutting out the full-back and into Spencer's path, but the Scot failed to score

With just minutes to go and the efforts of this typical Cup tie telling on his 33 year old legs, Gullit still had the energy to burst down the left flank and have his choice of players to pick out, selecting Petrescu who shot over. Then, another enticing pass to Petrescu, sending him clear down the right, as Chelsea threatened to finish off Rangers in a thrilling climax. It was nail-biting, but Chelsea chairman Ken Bates was wearing his lucky fur coat and the Blues scraped through!

Wilkins took responsibility for the penalty kick miss that cost QPR at least a chance of taking this tie to a replay. Wilkins said: 'There was practically fisticuffs in the dressing room afterwards between Mark Hateley and Trevor Sinclair about who should have taken it. I think had we scored from the spot we would have gone on to win the game. But Bradley is distraught about the miss without me adding salt to the wound. Nobody is a designated penalty kick taker, it was up to whoever most fancied it. He felt confident enough to take it and that's why he went to pick up the ball. But at the end I would rather take the stick than anyone else. And, of course, I'll accept the criticism when it comes. It's not very pleasant to be second to the bottom of the table and out of the Cup. I doesn't bother me that Bradley missed it. I just felt for him and not for myself.'

In the fifth round, the Cup tie at Grimsby took on even extra significance, Chelsea's entire season hinged on it. In a week in which they had lost at Coventry and then to West Ham, it was suggested to Hoddle that the same fate awaited them at Grimsby. 'We'll knock the third one on the head!' But he conceded: 'They are a very good footballing side, as West Ham found out, and it's going to be a tough game for us.' Gullit's presence was crucial as Hoddle added: 'Whoever you are, the motivation is the Cup final and Wembley. We went to Newcastle and won and our attitude for Grimsby is the same. The only thing that matters in the FA Cup is the two teams who finish at Wembley. Going out now means nothing.'

Chelsea halted the mini-slump in the league with a goalless draw at Grimsby, but they had to dig deep for survival to keep their FA Cup dream alive. The London side responded to the questions asked of their character and commitment to produce a brave and battling display. It was not the kind of match that Hoddle will look back on with affection for the quality of football. But he was satisfied how his team refused to buckle when Grimsby's football was at its most passionate. In the bad old days, Chelsea would not have survived the fever of Grimsby's play. Chelsea's Cup record is littered with desperate defeats, but now they kept their composure and defended with defiance when Grimsby's pressure might have overwhelmed them. Hoddle packed the midfield with players prepared to do a hard night's work, and Gullit once again played his part. He continually found the space and offered himself as the midfield mainspring to keep Chelsea ticking over.

However, Gullit was only able to control the game for the first 15 minutes until Grimsby hustled him out of his cultured stride. Captain Dennis Wise pointed out that Gullit's performance might have had something to do with the surreal surroundings and humble environment of Blundell Park. Wise said: 'I don't think he had seen anything quite like the away team's dressing room.'

Grimsby player-manager Brian Laws said: 'If anybody deserved to win, it was us. We showed Chelsea how to play. They couldn't get the ball off us. We'll give them another tough game and it's not over yet.' Grimsby's last run to the quarter-finals in 1939 included a victory over Chelsea, and they were out to claim another Premiership scalp following their impressive fourth round triumph over West Ham.

The thrill of the FA Cup was once again to inspire Ruud. Hoddle stressed before the fifth round replay at the Bridge that Gullit and Hughes were key players once again. 'I said when I signed them that they are winners, and they have had a huge part to play in getting that across to the other players. They are never satisfied with winning one thing. Like the great Liverpool sides of the past, they immediately start thinking about the next honour. When I was a player, I remember sitting in the dressing room at Wembley after winning the FA Cup with Spurs for the first time and thinking, 'This is great but I want more'. That is the sort of winning mentality you need – you are never satisfied.'

After three goals in four minutes devastated Grimsby, it was showtime at the Bridge As Chelsea passed the ball around extravagantly, defenders indulged themselves with overhead kicks, while Gullit danced on the touchline waving his hands over his head in an attempt to attract the ball. In between was breathtaking movement, and hold up play by Mark Hughes. It took just 23 minutes to get the first goal, and to pick up the heartbeat of a victory that was ultimately both comfortable and convincing. A move of shattering simplicity tore Grimsby apart. John Spencer knocked a long ball to Dan Petrescu who quickly switched it into the middle were Mike Duberry was there to head his first goal for the Blues from six yards. In the 55th minute Gullit picked out Gavin Peacock, he crossed, and Hughes drove his header past the keeper. To Grimsby's credit they came surging back, and 60 seconds later Paul Groves volleyed a fine goal. Chelsea set about the task with a will to win, that was totally ruthless. It was as if they suddenly changed into a higher gear, as two more goals came in two incredible minutes. First Wise set up Spencer in the 57th minute, and then two minutes later Peacock hit a right footer that took a deflection past keeper Paul Crichton. In that brilliant spell, Chelsea were unplayable.

But there was no euphoria from Ruud, only realism. 'We haven't won anything yet. At the moment there is nothing to celebrate. We're just a round further. You only have that feeling when you are part of the main event, the final. Until then, every game is just that – another game.' Ruud's influence on players such as Duberry was evident, his personal ambition trails behind a genuine desire to improve others. Alarmed at how the 20-year-old defensive find of the season had dipped in recent matches, Gullit took him aside and talked him back into form. His reward was Duberry's first goal for the club. 'He didn't know what was going on. He's a young guy, just got a new contract, sponsors and all the attention. I told him it was normal and it happens to everyone. I just talked to him and I was so happy for him that he had a good game. For two weeks he had not been the same as earlier in the season. But against Grimsby he did well and afterwards he was smiling. David Lee has done well, so has John Spencer, and Dennis

Wise. As a team we are more consistent now. We had a lot of ups and downs in the beginning and then we had a good run.'

Now Chelsea faced a crunching double header against Wimbledon in the league at Selhurst Park and then the Cup at the Bridge a week later. Gullit's first meeting with the Crazy Gang ended badly enough, with Vinny Jones sent off and later fined £2000 for accusing the Dutchman of conning the referee. But Ruud has too much experience to be disturbed by a rematch: 'Every team has its own style – I've played so many games like that. When we played Red Star one of my team-mates was put in hospital because he swallowed his tongue after being elbowed. You just have to cope and I have a lot of experience to do that.'

Hoddle camouflaged his Cup tactics by selecting an unusual side for the league encounter with the Dons at Selhurst Park. He left John Spencer and Gavin Peacock on the bench and went for height in attack with Paul Furlong. Chelsea went ahead against the run of play through Furlong in the move of the match – a well worked free-kick. As all eyes watched Gullit making a dummy run, Petrescu slipped the ball to Wise and the cross was perfect for Furlong. Marcus Gayle forced Wimbledon's equaliser with a low cross that Steve Clarke turned into his own net under pressure from Efan Ekoku.

Dons skipper Vinny Jones, who constantly ordered his colleagues to dull Gullit's fire, said: 'Hoddle flattered us by changing tactics and obviously trying to keep something back for next Saturday's Cup tie. We've also got a surprise or two left, but fair play to the man. He did well. It's a great pleasure playing against Gullit. Yet on Sunday morning, I'll be out sticking my hand up the backside of a sheep on my farm. It's lambing time. What a contrast. Close to Gullit's backside one day. Any one of 17 sheep another!'

Then to the FA Cup showdown with Wimbledon. There had

been no sign of the excitement to come in a lacklustre first half which saw Chelsea, in particular, not prepared to take any chances. Chelsea's back three were confused early on, although the loss of David Lee with sickness on the morning of the match did not help. Gullit was in a quiet mood during the opening exchanges, but the fireworks finally started ten minutes into the second half when Duberry became the first player to receive a booking from referee Graham Poll. From the free-kick by Jones, Earle beat the Chelsea defence to the ball to head Wimbledon in front. Then, Wise delivered a curling cross which Furlong got to first. Although his shot came off the post, it fell to Hughes who was able to run it into the net. Chelsea took the lead, following a free-kick when Wimbledon were penalised because Sullivan was harassed by Spencer into handling the ball from a back pass. Wise tapped the free-kick on the edge of the box to Gullit, whose blaster hit Jones standing in the wall and the ball was deflected into the net. As Wimbledon so often do, the equaliser came immediately. This time Kimble's free-kick found Holdsworth, who made it 2–2, and the replay was set up.

Big, bruising centre-forward Mick Harford, who had been substituted, was ever-combative, even when on the bench. He is alleged to have told Hoddle: 'Justice is done. You obviously sorted the ref out on your side.' Hoddle, unsurprisingly, took exception and exchanged words with Joe Kinnear afterwards. With Chelsea fans joining in verbally, an excellent Cup tie ended angrily. It was an outrageous verbal tirade at the Chelsea manager. Harford also infuriated fans with a V-sign as he was substituted in the 77th minute.

'Harford's language was atrocious towards Glenn,' said Chelsea's safety officer Keith Lacy who heard the volley of words from his vantage point near the dug-outs. 'Harford simply lost his rag.' The flashpoint was Mr Poll's 80th minute decision to award

Chelsea a free-kick for what he judged to be a deliberate back pass by Kenny Cunningham to keeper Neil Sullivan. From the free-kick, Chelsea scored.

Poll, who had averaged five bookings a game and has in past matches sent off three Wimbledon players, said: 'I saw nothing wrong with what Harford did. In fact, I wasn't even aware of anything taking place.'

Kinnear said: 'Mick was very upset that we only got a draw, and so were a lot of us. Mick said to Hoddle, 'I suppose you've sorted out the referee on your side'. Glenn was upset about that. But I can understand Mick's feelings as well. We were judged to have given away a back pass and they scored. I've always thought the rules stated that it has to be intent. I shall be asking the Referees' Association for a clear definition. We certainly won't be asking for Mr Poll to be replaced in the replay. We have every faith in him and we do not want to inflame the situation any more.'

Harford tried to play down the incident: 'Nothing happened. It was all quiet. No problem.'

You cannot get away from controversy where Wimbledon are concerned! But Kinnear was more anxious that his side should be given credit for a superb fighting draw. 'We believed we could upset them and we nearly did. Our job was to put pressure on their back four and it almost worked out.'

Harford's fate was sealed by the fourth official Peter Jones. Poll did not see the incident but it was witnessed by Loughborough-based Jones, a Premiership referee. The FA confirmed that Chelsea managing director Colin Hutchinson had been in touch with Lancaster Gate to inquire about the FA's position on the incident. Harford was charged with misconduct by the FA. The 37-year-old forward was in trouble for an alleged V-sign to Chelsea supporters, rather than the reported verbal assault on Hoddle. Although the fourth official witnessed the scenes, he did not hear what was said, but did see Harford make the gesture to Chelsea fans. 'Mick Harford has been charged with misconduct for giving a two-fingered gesture to the crowd when he was substituted during Saturday's Cup tie,' confirmed the FA. Chelsea faced a fierce backlash at Selhurst Park as Wimbledon were furious that attempts were made to get Harford in trouble.

For the replay there was concern over Gullit's attempts to recover from flu. He had been ordered back to bed on the eve of the quarter-final replay. His worried manager gave him until lunchtime of the day of the game to prove his fitness. 'You want a player of Ruud's stature in a Cup game like this,' Hoddle said. 'We put vitamins down him all weekend and he's had enough sleep. But we put vitamins down him and he didn't make it at Liverpool. When he tried to train today, it took a lot out of him and he's been sent back to bed. Craig Burley came in at the weekend against Liverpool and did very well after cartilage operations on both knees, but we'll have to wait and see how Ruud is before we leave for the match. We'll make a decision as late as possible but he looks a major doubt at the moment.'

Wimbledon believed it was all kidology over Gullit. 'We think it's all a bit of gamesmanship because, although flu can make you weak, I'm certain he'll be out there,' said Dons' full-back Kenny Cunningham. 'I have heard what Hoddle said about Ruud being in bed sneezing. Glenn Hoddle is trying get it into our heads that Gullit won't be playing so that when we see his name on the team-sheet an hour before kick-off, we think 'Oh my God he is playing'. To be honest I'd be very surprised if Gullit doesn't play.'

Hoddle said: 'The past two meetings between us and Wimbledon have been very tight and I don't suppose this one will be any different. But we are going there feeling very confident because I have told the boys if we can win at Newcastle, we can win anywhere.'

Finally, Chelsea overcame Wimbledon. Gullit may have failed to score at Selhurst Park but the night was laced with the special brand of skill and intelligence he has brought to Chelsea's football. Hoddle said: 'I told the players to give it to him, to feet, and when we did Wimbledon couldn't live with him. If you get the ball down you can pass it on any surface – even one as difficult as this. Ruud was coughing and spluttering in the hotel before the game. He hadn't felt well at training and I'm not sure he would have lasted extra-time.'

It was certainly a dramatic quarter-final replay. The prize could not have been bigger... Manchester Unites in the semis. Hoddle gasped: 'There were so many stories out there – three in particular when you have Mike Duberry scoring his first Cup goal, then you have Romanian Dan Petrescu hoping for a Wembley final and then of course there's Mark Hughes dreaming of Wembley yet again and beating his old club. It was a tremendous night for everyone.'

Hoddle gambled on Gullit, still recovering from a heavy cold. 'His run to provide the cross for Mark's goal was worth watching alone.'

Kinnear was sporting in defeat. 'It was a cracking tie. I felt that both teams made a real go of it. Chelsea took their chances and we didn't. We went to sleep when Duberry scored and I believe that was the crucial moment. I've spoken to my team in the dressing room and hopefully I've picked them up. I told them they were magnificent.'

Dan Petrescu put Chelsea ahead after 21 minutes when he drove home from a difficult angle after being put clear by Craig Burley. The Romanian's shot whistled into the far corner. Wise gave his former Wimbledon mates a let-off with a dreadfully weak penalty four minutes later after Petrescu had been brought down by Alan Kimble. Then Gullit hit the post from 25 yards, with Sullivan beaten. It was all knife-edge stuff and Wimbledon equalised in the 41st minute when a devastating Ekoku cross from the right offered Jon Goodman the chance to head home.

Wimbledon continually tried to exploit Chelsea's weakness in central defence and were riding high until Wise and Gullit began to orchestrate a revival. It was pulsating action. Gullit sprayed the ball with class while Wise fought out a ferocious midfield battle with his best pal Vinny Jones. Harford and Wise were booked by referee Graham Poll as the temperature rose on an icy cold night.

Duberry, who bears a remarkable resemblance to Mike Tyson – hence his nickname 'Iron Mike' – broke the deadlock of a nail-biting replay. His 80th-minute header from a John Spencer cross unlocked a battle royal and Hughes then put the game beyond the battling Dons. Hughes finished a move he began deep into his own half. He switched passes with Gullit before touching in the Dutchman's cross six minutes from time. The Chelsea contingent within a 21,000 crowd exploded into relieved acclamation of a third major semi-final in successive seasons.

Wimbledon sank to their knees in despair as Hoddle pulled Gullit from the battlefield to a tremendous reception. It was the last of many inspirational interventions from the Dutchman. That he had so much running in him at the end of a gruelling match, on a heavy pitch, was nothing short of a marvel, given that he had been a doubtful starter because of flu.

'I told the lads to get the ball to Ruud, from throw-ins and corners, whenever they could, because the opposition couldn't live with him,' smiled Hoddle.

Chelsea now faced Manchester United in the semi-final. Mark Hughes was looking forward to taking on his old club. He believed the clash between the Gullit and Eric Cantona would be one of the highlights of the season. There is no one better equipped than Hughes to compare the merits of the Dutchman and the Frenchman. Hughes, who won the Cup three times at United, said: 'They both have enormous presence, they are both world-class players and I feel very fortunate to have been able to play with both of them. You saw in our victory at Wimbledon that Ruud's performance was out of this world especially considering he has been ill for a couple of days. To come back and perform like that was nothing short of fantastic. But that's the way he's been all season. He is very difficult to shake off the ball because he is such a big man and he has pace, strength, and a natural footballing ability. When you put all those together he's quite a package. He's a lot louder than Eric, he never stops talking. They have different styles and it is difficult to compare but you have to judge them by the influence they have had on their sides this season. They've brought great things to our game and if we keep attracting players like them everyone else can only improve.'

Hughes, who helped destroy Chelsea at Wembley to complete the Double two years ago, added: 'Chelsea are a much better side now. There's a lot of players who have been around a bit, me included. The likes of Ruud, Dan Petrescu and Terry Phelan have a lot of experience and they know that in certain situations, you must not panic, just keep your nerve.' Unfortunately Petrescu, a vital part of Chelsea's new look team, was ruled out through suspension.

At the semi-final at Villa Park, there was no cooler customer for such a big game than Ruud Gullit. Only when you've been voted the World's Best Player, and appeared in European Cup finals as Gullit has, can you say of an FA Cup semi-final: 'It means nothing.' It was not his intention to sound disrespectful but, as he says: 'It's not an achievement, you don't get a medal for it. The only thing that matters is to play in the final – and win it. I know the FA Cup final would be a special occasion, but I never thought of the European Cup final until we were there. The strange thing is that in the moment you win it you get an explosion of joy, but the next day you have something else to think about. I remember with Milan, we won the European Cup at Barcelona and three days after that I had to prepare myself for the European Championships, so you begin again at zero. You just forget what you've done and focus yourself on something new because if you don't perform well, you get hammered as if that thing you achieved a few days before did not even happen. That's life; if you are on the highest level. You cannot think about standing still on what you have achieved, you must go further all the time. The only moment when you can sit down and relax is when you retire. Then you can say that was great.'

With such an outlook it is little wonder he enquires: 'What is the semi-final?' Not out of arrogance but a charming certainty of what matters in life. He explained: 'Only the final is special. The only thing that matters is to play in the final and also to win it. Chelsea have been there and lost it so they know what it means.' As for the semi-final … 'I just want to enjoy myself,' he says.

Alex Ferguson paid Ruud the ultimate tribute in the big build up to the match. He rated him in the world's top ten: 'He's been a big, big influence on the Chelsea team. It definitely wasn't a case of him being here for a nice little rest. He's showed that in all the games he's played in, he's played with desire. I think great players are great players until they pack up. He'll be classed in the top ten players of the last decade. He's right up there.'

Ruud and Chelsea were clear outsiders, and that view was shared by the media. Yet, there was no doubt among the experts that Gullit would make a vital contribution to the event. Rob Hughes, of *The Times* wrote: 'Ruud Gullit fibs about it; Eric Cantona says nothing about it; and both crave it down to their boots. Their teams, Chelsea and Manchester United, are one giant stride from the FA Cup final at Wembley. When they meet at Villa Park in their semi-final, you can be sure they will have the twin towers on their minds. It is part of their becoming Anglicised, part of the dream of childhood well beyond these shores. It is the final of all finals and Gullit is simply giving a cliché in another accent when he says that the game is nothing special to him. Those who know him well know for certain that the romance moves him. At 33, he is playing for an opportunity that may never come again, and if, for a moment, you did strip away the pageant, brought it down to basics, it is a fact that reaching Wembley would compensate Chelsea with the entire £1.6 million that the club reputedly pays him in salary. Yet what part will Gullit and Cantona play? Of all the 147 foreigners so rapidly integrated into the English game, they are the most influential.'

Typically, Ruud dismissed the hype of a personal contest with Cantona. 'The comparison between us is not interesting for me because I know the game is not going to be resolved by two players. The game will be resolved by team performance. I respect Manchester United very much. They have good skills, good players, and you know what they can do. They can be very clinical. They go 1–0 up and they close the door. They can do this because they have a lot of experience in the team.' Ruud felt there was little point in trying to stifle Cantona, just one individual in a team packed full of star performers. 'If you have one person marking him, who is not free to look around, then you have only 10 players and they have 11. We have to play a good game as a team so that they can't put him in the right position, that's the point. We can perform well against United. Our main opponent will be ourselves.'

In reality, Gullit was Chelsea's best chance of success. Coach Peter Shreeves said: 'In the last five weeks he's been marvellous. He alone got us through that Wimbledon tie, pulling us up by our bootlaces. He also gives us an extra threat around goal. When he's got the ball 35 yards from goal you always think he is going to dip his shoulder and move off. He's still got pace to go past people.'

Chelsea fans travelled to the Midlands in their droves, convinced this would be their Gullit inspired season and, even though outnumbered by the United contingent, they backed their team to such an extent their singing of the 'Blue Flag' drowned out the announcer reading the Manchester United line-up. Ferguson marched on to the pitch to urge his fans for more support!

After just five minutes Ryan Giggs whipped over a tantalising low cross that Londoner David Beckham struck against the post from close range, with a well executed side-foot shot. Inevitably Gullit raised the Chelsea standard, linking up with full-back Steve Clarke, whose shot dipped just over. Defender Michael Duberry unleashed a left footed curler that struck the underside of the bar when he spotted Schmeichel off his line. There was little evidence of Chelsea's sweet passing game on an atrocious surface. With United clear favourites Chelsea needed to grab the initiative and the only route was via a goal as United dominated the early exchanges.

Gullit delivered, opening the scoring after 35 minutes. Hughes was the instigator battling bravely, as usual, against Phil Neville and Beckham enabling Spencer to get a touch. There was a hint of Hughes holding back Beckham before getting to the by-line, his perfect cross to the far post headed in by the dreadlocked player quoted at 10–1 to score the first goal.

Next a Gullit 20 yarder flashed just wide but Cantona surpassed it with a wonderful volley timed so perfectly. It was struck with venomous power but it hit the same upright that saved Kevin Hitchcock from an early Beckham strike. Chelsea gave Manchester United a far tougher time than when they eventually capitulated 4–0 in the final two years earlier.

The turning point came with a rare Cole goal – his first for five weeks. But in reality Cantona's header would probably have crossed the line when Cole interceded, athletically raising his foot to ensure the equaliser in the 55th minute. Phil Neville got to the by-line and his deep cross was edged on to the back post by David Lee, where Cantona stretched to his limits to reach his header and give Cole an easy tap in. Four minutes later Craig Burley's over elaborate attempt to clear his lines ended with a disastrous back pass that Beckham gobbled up with a shot in the corner. Burley tried to make amends with a long ball, just after the hour, that Gullit turned into a genuine chance, utilising his strength against May to get a touch that would have been good enough for an equaliser but Schmeichel smothered it. Spencer latched on to the rebound but Cantona's awareness took him to the goalline where he stopped the Scot's shot with his head. Gullit wasn't finished, despite the amount of energy he used up, laying on a guilt edged chance for skipper Dennis Wise in the 76th minute. Gullit's pass was inch perfect into the path of Wise, but his shot was brilliantly saved by Schmeichel.

It would have been fitting for Cantona to have rounded off his superlative performance with a goal, but five minutes from the end the Frenchman's header was acrobatically saved by Hitchcock, and Cole's shot from the rebound was hooked off the line by Andy Myers.

Ruud was bidding to become the first player to win the Cup in three different countries, having already tasted Cup final glory in Holland and Italy. He did all he could to take Chelsea to Wembley, not just for himself but for the entire team, but it wasn't to be. Alex Ferguson danced on the Villa Park pitch in an exhibition of undiluted delight; they say FA Cup semi-final losers are instantly forgotten but before the Manchester United boss cuddled his hero Eric Cantona, he wrapped his arms around Ruud Gullit.

At the end even the Manchester United fans applauded Gullit, as well as their former idol Mark Hughes, off the Villa Park pitch. For once the memories will linger upon a side that fell in an FA Cup semi-final. Mainly for the riveting contribution of Gullit and the irrepressible desire to beat his old club from Hughes. Gullit is sportsmanship personified. Even the bitterness of failure did not deter him from reciprocating the Manchester United fans appreciation of his skills by applauding them as he left the field. It was a moving experience for Gullit. 'Very emotional', he said. 'I was doing everything possible to get us into the final. We were so close as well.'

A close-up of Gullit's personal performance shows just how hard he worked to fulfil Chelsea's dream of a Wembley appearance:

2nd min: A neat lay off to Wise and he was on his way with just that simple, yet beautiful touch.

5th min: Gullit embarks on a brilliant run down the touch line leaving youngster Nicky Butt in his tracks to the backdrop of deafening noise.

13th min: Clarke plays a game of one-two with Gullit who returns the favour for the Chelsea defender to shoot just over.

17th min: Gullit shows his incredible will to win when he takes on a defensive role to cut out a Cole pass and then spreads the ball out wide to Spencer at the start of another blistering move.

35th min: Hughes scraps for his life and delivers the perfect pass for Ruud to head home for the opener.

37th min: Gullit bustles past Cole, strong enough to finish with a drive that flashes a foot wide.

38th min: Gullit in the thick of the action again and only a despairing lunge by David May saves the day.

60th min: Ruud sneaks in ahead of May and pokes the ball forward only to see Schmeichel spread himself wide and stop him.

76 min: Gullit refuses to give up the fight and rolls the ball into Wise's path only for Schmeichel to block and then watch Gullit's bullet shot whistle by.

78th min: Wise lifts a free-kick for Gullit to ease into the area and Spencer nearly grabs the equaliser.

90th min: It's all over and Gullit reserves a special hug for his fellow maestro Cantona.

Hoddle clashed angrily with television pundit Alan Hansen after the former Liverpool defender claimed the Chelsea manager's tactics regarding injured Terry Phelan cost him a chance of reaching the FA Cup final. Phelan soldiered on for 20 minutes after suffering an injury, and in that time Andy Cole and David Beckham both scored. Hansen claimed Hoddle should have taken Phelan off immediately but the Stamford Bridge boss said: 'That's Alan's point of view. Until he sits in the dugout and finds out about it himself he's welcome to his views.' Hoddle, who had already lost his other full-back Steve Clarke, added: 'Terry felt he could play on, that it was just a slight thing. If a player says he thinks he can continue you listen, especially when you've lost one full-back and don't really want to reshape both flanks so early in the game. It's just unfortunate we've had to use players in those positions who have never played there, and in the end it turned the game. But you must find out whether the player can continue or not, and it's just unfortunate that in that time you conceded a crucial goal. If I'd had a left back on the bench I would have made the decision a lot quicker, that's for sure.'

Gullit refused to toe the party line almost all foreign players tread when they come to play in England. He insisted: 'Just one match at Wembley is not so important to me as seeing this Chelsea team develop and taking shape in the way we want. I'm disappointed we got so close and didn't make it to Wembley but playing in the FA Cup final was not a particular goal of mine. I have sympathy for the players but you can't afford to have just one goal to achieve. I said this even before the semi-final and I feel no differently now. I'm looking to achieve much more with Chelsea and I'm happy with the way we are going. There can be too much attention on one match and it can affect your overall aim. That was the case against Manchester United and we lost because of two points – injuries and the fact that we created two goals for them that they didn't create themselves. It was a pity but we will be better for the experience. Maybe we will be a little more cynical in the future when we are in the lead.'

Gullit was also first to console the distraught Craig Burley. Gullit said: 'I went to Burley straight after Manchester scored and told him not to worry. We did not lose just because he made one mistake. When we win, we win together and when we lose it is together also. He played very well – and it could have been me who made that mistake on another occasion. He was very, very upset. But he did his best, no-one could ask for more. He also played a big part in our win against Wimbledon to help us get to the semi-final. For me, the result depended on two episodes – the injuries to Steve Clarke and Terry Phelan and the goals. One chance in a game like this can be vital. With good strikers, give them one chance and they score.'

Ruud concluded: 'We now have to learn from the semi-final. I am happy with the team and with the players we have got and we can get better from this season. If there was a lesson, it is that you cannot afford to make mistakes at this level. But Chelsea played well.'

CHAPTER SEVEN

The Troubleshooter

Ruud Gullit is no ordinary footballer. He has a mind of his own – and for a start that puts him apart from most of his fellow professionals! A footballer with opinions is bound to attract controversy, especially when it comes from one of the world's greatest ever performers. His views within the Dutch World Cup camp were to lead to an amazing bust up before World Cup '94 in America, when Gullit stormed out only weeks before the tournament was due to begin, refusing to ever play again for his country. There can be few more controversial things to do than that!

No matter how hard Ruud Gullit tries to be a diplomat, controversy is never far away. Ruud came to England with a reputation as a troubleshooter. Certainly, he showed his courage to take on important issues when, just a couple of months after arriving in England, he was prepared to put his name and his formidable presence to the campaign against racism at a high level press conference at Wembley on 28 September. Ruud joined with leading players to launch the latest stage of a campaign against racism and intimidation in English football under the new slogan: 'Respect All Fans.'

Arsenal and England captain Tony Adams, John Barnes and Gary Lineker united with Gullit in the campaign backed by the

FA. Its aim was to raise public awareness of the damaging effects of racism and intimidatory behaviour on the image of the game. Ken Bates applauded Gullit 'for doing more to help race relations at Chelsea than dozens of other people put together.'

Ruud said: 'People shouting and swearing at you has been accepted as part of the game, but should it be? The players can play their part in making sure children know the standards of behaviour we should all be aiming for. I'm aware of racism everywhere. I believe it's not only black and white but male and female, rich and poor. It is society's problem. So far it has been good over here. It's not been the image you're fed in Italy. The regular hooligans don't exist. Italy only sees them when England is abroad. But they're not supporters, not anything to do with the regular supporters who are turning up here.'

The campaign was intriguingly timed with the return of Eric Cantona from his nine month ban. Ruud urged Cantona to use racist taunts as ammunition to fuel his comeback. Ruud has had to suffer his share of abuse from rival supporters in Holland, Italy and now England and he fears Cantona is also targeted. 'If someone is booing me I take it as a compliment because they are afraid of me. It makes me play better and that is what Eric must do. The whole world was shocked by what he did but we cannot keep dragging it up. If you are a foreigner playing well in another country, you are going to get a lot of attention. You just have to control yourself. We have to forgive him and hope that he has learned his lesson. We must consider him as a football player.'

In April 1996, Ruud was honoured with the role of European Ambassador for the campaign against racism and violence in football. Dutch Sports Minister Erica Terpstra said: 'We are thrilled that Ruud Gullit has agreed to lead this campaign. We could not have wished for a bigger sports personality in Europe to do this.'

Gullit has experienced the bigots in English football. He was shamelessly booed by the Boro fans at the opening of their plush new Riverside Stadium. The heckling of Gullit was a back-handed compliment, because he is the player the opposition fans feared the most. The *Daily Mirror* criticised the fans. North-East correspondent Colin Diball nominated them 'Moan of the Match'. He wrote: 'Why can't they appreciate such colossal talent?'

On another occasion Gullit suffered a hostile reception from QPR fans as he was caught in a 'diving' controversy. The crowd turned on him with chants of 'cheat' after he went down following a challenge by midfield player Ian Holloway. Referee David Elleray spoke to Holloway while QPR players protested his innocence. But for the rest of the game the crowd were on Gullit's back, booing him every time he touched the ball. Brian Scovell observed in the *Daily Mail*: 'English crowds have a strange way of appreciating the game's greats, or failing to appreciate them. The night before it was Eric Cantona who was abused by Tottenham fans. Gullit was even booed as he was carried off.'

Ruud was not surprised that Paul Furlong and Frank Sinclair had suffered racial taunts during Chelsea's trips abroad the previous season at Club Brugge and Real Zaragoza. He said: 'It happened also with Ajax in Hungary. Ajax reported it to UEFA. But UEFA had an official sitting in the stand who didn't write one word about it. It's become a habit for officials, I think which is not a good sign. If it happens, clubs must do something.'

Never afraid to stand up for his principles, Gullit can became an easy target and courted controversy on a number of occasions in his first season in English football.

The notorious former hod carrier Vinny Jones, never slow to make a name for himself with his outlandish actions, launched a scathing attack on Gullit. The Wimbledon hard man accused Gullit of being here only for the money. Jones blasted: 'He's here on a bus ride. He will go around, see the sights and say thanks very much. He's already said he doesn't want to play over Christmas. But this is England, he's on £20,000 a week and should just get on with it.' Gullit had been used to having Christmas and the New Year off, as is the custom in Italy when they shut down *Serie A* for a couple of weeks.

It was a ludicrous criticism, and condemned by Chelsea chief executive Colin Hutchinson in the club programme, who described it as outrageous. But it didn't end there with Jones. He 'charged' Gullit with diving and getting him sent off in the Boxing Day match that Chelsea lost 1–0 at the Bridge. The result was a genuine charge of misconduct for Jones from the FA, a guilty verdict and a hefty fine for his troubles.

The core of the argument began with Jones' dismissal in Wimbledon's win over Chelsea at the Bridge. Jones put another notch on the worst CV in soccer, this time his victim was Gullit. Despite more red cards than anyone still in the game, he protested his innocence even though TV evidence showed that Vinny was a sinner for the 11th time in his infamous career. Jones was sent off for two bookings – the second for a fierce challenge on Gullit that Jones insisted was fair.

Gullit fell backwards after a crunching tackle from behind by Jones. Gullit was kicked up in the air but Jones had the audacity to accuse him of diving. He snapped: 'Gullit is a class player and he's pulled the ball back. I slid in and I played the ball, the ball went straight into the crowd and I thought nothing of it. Even the Chelsea players couldn't believe it when I was sent off, but I was punished for Gullit's dive. The only thing Gullit did in the game was get me and Mick Harford booked.'

Hoddle said: 'It's always somebody else's fault.' Jones was

shown the red card – his third of the season – and left the field with a few choice words aimed at Hoddle in the Chelsea dug-out before heading for the dressing room. Hoddle added: 'I can't see how Jones can have any complaints. He went in with two rash tackles. When you've been booked once you have to change your game, but that's a lesson for him to learn.'

Jones, first booked for a lunging tackle on Dan Petrescu, insisted that Gullit was to blame: 'Eight or nine of our boys said it was a good tackle and even the Chelsea players said that I played the ball. I heard John Spencer and David Lee say it straight away. If it had been Mark Hughes he would have battled through, got up and got on with it. If this one was reckless I'd have put my foot out and shown my studs. Instead I tried to get my legs out of the way and he went over on me.'

Gullit gave his side of the story: 'If someone wants to hit you in the face, and you see it coming, what do you do? You try and avoid it, don't you? It's the same in a game. When someone is coming at you with both feet, you have to go up in order to avoid the tackle. If you don't, he'll break your legs. Even when you jump, they still hit you, but it's not so bad. I said to him: 'If I stay on my feet what do you think will happen? You'd break my leg. Would you be happy then? I don't want you to get the red card, but I don't want a broken leg either. He accused me of diving when he didn't even hit me. But his attitude was wrong, so you have to punish his attitude.'

But Gullit showed disdain at the Jones incident. He said: 'The episode was not important, the game itself was important and I felt Wimbledon played a good game, and worked hard for it and wanted it. But as for the red card that is not so important and I'm not going to argue about something that's not important.'

Wimbledon manager Joe Kinnear said at the time: 'Vinny swears blind he made contact with the ball and that Ruud went over on top of him. That's his version I'm sure there will be another from Gullit. They all say in our dressing room it was a good tackle, but I want to look at the TV. Vinny's reputation seems to go before him and these things seem to continue to happen to him.'

But the real damage was done when Jones decided to add insult to injury, literally. In his *Daily Mirror* column on 28 December, Jones launched a venomous and unprovoked slur on Gullit's character that ultimately backfired on the tattooed clogger with an instant FA charge of disrepute. It wasn't hard to tell that it was ghost-written, but they were Jones' views and the article authorised by him.

'I own two pot-bellied pigs, yet they don't yelp as much as Ruud Gullit. Listen closely and you'll hear a new noise in football – it's called "The Foreign Squeal". It's the sound of money-grabbing imports dying on a bed of cash. And it could be the death knell of our game. Gullit, Juninho and other mega-stars have danced and pranced on British soccer. They've come here offering skill, most certainly, given dosh most definitely, but some have conned referees and the pot-bellied hacks who report on our Beautiful Game. Beautiful Game? What's beautiful about lying in mud and acting like a cockroach on its back. How does it feel, Ruud? He discovered a bit of mud on his socks and squealed. I still recall his voice. It was: "Oh, I'm not hurt, but I'll pretend to be if I get someone sent off or booked." It's a sound going round football ever since we allowed the Europeans to arrive.

'In the bar after Saturday's game I sensed disgust even from Chelsea players. They knew I had been wronged. David Lee and John Spencer both offered apologies for a dreadful decision. They weren't criticising Gullit, but just the general standard of refereeing. There's an ironic twist here, because I rate Dermot Gallagher one of my top five. He is a superb official. Yet I wonder sometimes did he book me twice because he wanted to, or because he was ordered by new rules. English soccer is determined to kill the tough tackle. Yet, managers, players and fans thrive on physical contact. Do we want basketball rules here? Of course not. Football is combat.'

Jones was charged with bringing the game into disrepute and disowned by his own club. The FA leapt in faster than a Vinny tackle with the charge. Neither Gullit nor Chelsea made an official complaint. But FA Chief executive Graham Kelly said: 'Personal attacks on fellow professionals are always likely to initiate a reaction from the FA.'

An FA spokesman said: 'All decent fans will acknowledge that overseas players have been a great benefit to the British game and generated a huge amount of interest. The quality of the Premier League has been enhanced by players like Dennis Bergkamp, Jurgen Klinsmann and Ruud Gullit. Vinny Jones will have 14 days to answer the charge and request a personal hearing.'

Wimbledon issued a statement saying: 'We believe the referee had no alternative but to take the action he did. We have stood by Vinny in the past when we felt he was being unfairly treated. But it is not something we do blindly. Vinny let himself down, the rest of the team and the whole club and must accept the consequences.'

Hoddle insisted that nobody at Chelsea had asked for Jones to be charged with bringing the game into disrepute for his comments about Gullit. But he said: 'Jones can have no complaints. I don't even want to talk about him. We should be talking about people who caress the ball and play positive football, not people who just do negative things.'

Jones was savagely criticised; even by the man who helped make him a cult figure in soccer. Wimbledon owner Sam Hammam put the boot in. Jones was left to face the music alone. He pledged not to dispute the disrepute charge. Hammam, who has loyally defended Jones over the years, also confirmed the club won't appeal against his sending off at Chelsea on Boxing Day. Hammam said: 'This is not the Vinny Jones I know and whom I regarded as almost a son.' He added: 'I feel Vinny has let everyone down very badly. He has let down Ruud Gullit, Joe, me, the club, his football family and, indeed, his family. Let's get it straight, Ruud Gullit did not take a dive and this attack on him should never have happened. It does not reflect on his wonderful character. Ruud Gullit is gracing English football, and foreign players in general are a major asset to the English game.'

Now it was Jones' turn to squeal like a pig! He said: 'I hold up my hands and apologise for calling Ruud a "squealer". I was angry, frustrated at being sent off and having 50 reporters knocking at my door for a reaction. I hit out. Ruud took the blows. I went over the top. I still believe he did go down hard, did make a meal of it. But a bloke of his genius deserves more than being called a 'squealer' and a 'cockroach'. For that I am deeply sorry. I know it was wrong on my part to attack a fellow pro – although there have been a few who had a go at me and got away with it – but I needed to get it off my chest. Attacking Ruud was wrong. Having a go at the system was right. This will be my defence. Hopefully, sanity will prevail.'

Dennis Bergkamp, on the eve of facing Wimbledon, couldn't hide his anger at the way Jones had criticised Gullit. Bergkamp said: 'Ruud has won more medals than Jones has red cards. If he has a problem with Ruud, he should say it to his face. It's easy to talk about other players, but the best way to get along in football is to achieve. I know Ruud and he hates people rolling around every time they are touched. One of the reasons we came to play in England is because players are so honest and don't take a dive as much. Everyone is entitled to an opinion in football, but not necessarily if it means criticising a fellow player in public. Jones should have said something to Ruud after the game in the players' lounge. Ruud is a great thinker about the game and prefers to talk about these things face-to-face. I know, from playing in Italian football with him, how much he dislikes players rolling over and then getting up and sprinting away a few seconds later. The Germans have even invented their own word for it. I have never liked that aspect of the game on the Continent and what I like about the game in England is that it is more fair.'

Joe Kinnear labelled Jones a reckless fool but the Wimbledon manager refused to jettison his skipper, he said: 'Vinny is sometimes his own worst enemy. I put my arm around him today and said 'You're a twit. You don't slag off blokes like Gullit – even if you feel you are right'. I said 'How many World Cups have you been in?' He realised what I meant.'

The critics condemned Jones. None more savagely than the *Mail on Sunday's* columnist Patrick Collins. 'The tackle was vicious and the subsequent insults were predictably lurid, but it was Vinny Jones' attempt to say sorry to Ruud Gullit which will linger longest in the memory ... So miffed was he at his latest misfortune that he lent his name to an odious piece of xenophobia which somehow encompassed foreigners in general, Gullit in particular, and Vinny's own pot-bellied pigs.'

Johnny Giles in the *Daily Express* wrote: 'It pains me to refer to Vinny Jones. I've never considered him a serious footballer. He has been a clever charlatan, exploiting a desperate poverty in English football ... Jones' offences against Dan Petrescu and Ruud Gullit were wretched examples of him taking advantage of players unprepared for such fouls. In the old days, everyone knew the score. And an alleged hardman like Jones, who is so tentative in 50–50 tackles, would have been laughed out of the game.'

Jones delivered a hand-written letter of apology to the FA for his criticisms of Gullit. He said: 'I was asked to explain my comments and wrote back to them to apologise and express my deep regret at making my remarks in public. I have got to be man enough to admit my mistakes and I hope that will be taken into consideration when the case comes to be decided.' Jones declined a personal hearing to challenge the disrepute charge. 'I am sure the disciplinary committee will deal with the matter fairly.' Jones was subsequently fined £2,000. It was the fifth substantial fine in the past three years.

The Jones controversy was nothing compared to the New Year furore that exploded when Ruud's observations about the standard of British players in an Italian newspaper were translated, regurgitated, and misrepresented in the English press. Ruud's views on English football were reproduced on 3rd January with devastating effect. But the way his opinions were interpreted bitterly upset Ruud.

Ruud was supposed to have said that he felt English stars are still way behind their counterparts in Italy. He suggested that any *Serie A* player would make a name for himself in England, while he has seen only three Premiership players capable of making an impact with the Italians. 'There are not many here I would consider for Italy although I particularly like the look of Ryan Giggs, Les Ferdinand and Robbie Fowler. It is hard in Italy. Not just for individuals like Paul Ince, who it seems is not doing very well, but for everyone – even the current champions Juventus. All of those in Italy could play in England. I'm not joking – all of them. The most important and best football is played in Italy. Someone like Marco Simone at AC Milan would be top scorer straight away if he came to England and he would do really well at Liverpool. They are a good team.'

Ruud completely refuted that he said anything of the sort. His misinterpreted comments provoked a huge volume of outrage. 'I was asked if there were any players in the Premiership who were good enough to play in Italy. I named three, but I could have named twenty. The press claimed that I said that there were *only* three English players good enough. It just goes to prove that someone in my position has to be careful of what they say.'

Sir Bobby Charlton was stirred to bang the drum for English footballers. Sir Bobby said: 'Our football is packed with exciting players who could more than hold their own in Italy – and anywhere else in the world.'

Gullit picked out Giggs, Ferdinand and Fowler. Sir Bobby agreed with that assessment. 'He's right about those three – they are all gifted. But there are plenty of others'

Brian Roy, who played for Foggia in Italy before his £2.6 million move to Nottingham Forest, said: 'There is a tremendous amount of talent in the English league. People in this country should not be as quick as they seem to be to under-estimate it. Foreign players obviously find it hard going in Italian football, which is very technical, but it can be very demanding coming here too. That's not just because of the extra pace in the game in England. There are a lot of very gifted players as well.'

Les Ferdinand knows Ruud better to believe that the Dutchman was so critical of the English game. He was 'flattered' to win the Gullit seal of approval but added: 'You only have to look at the Newcastle team to see there are players like Peter Beardsley and Robert Lee who could perform well in Italy. I know Ruud and I know what he's like. I'm taking this with a pinch of salt because I don't think he's the sort to have a go at the English game. There are plenty of quality players around in England. A lot of foreign players want to play here because it's the best league in the world. I accept that the success rate of English players abroad is not that great. But there's a lot more to it than simply playing football in a foreign country. You have to learn to adapt as well and that's not always easy.'

Ian Rush who spent a season with Juventus, insists Italian players would have far more trouble adapting to the English game than vice-versa. He said: 'I've seen both sides and without a doubt the Italians would find it hard to cope with the physical nature of our football, the speed of the game and the number of matches we play. Skill-wise, I would accept we are not as good as the Continentals, but in Italy you have more time to show off your skill, especially at the back and in midfield, because the game is slower. In English football, whatever part of the pitch you are in, it is all 100 mph. Gullit has made a harsh verdict on our League for the simple reason it's so much faster and harder than the Italian League. I don't think anyone can argue that our League is best for excitement. You would never have seen a game like Liverpool v Forest on New Year's Day in Italy.'

Johnny Metgod the former Forest and Spurs hero now Youth Development Officer at Feyenoord, backed Gullit's verdict on the Premiership. 'If you look at skill and technique then Ruud is probably correct. He is especially right about the defences. I am not putting anybody down, just being realistic. He has played in *Serie A* and I have not, so he is a better judge than me. I would say there are a few more than just three players who could make it in Italy, but not many more than that.' Metgod said that the signs are that the English game will change. He said: 'There is a lot of talk about a change of system and style of play, especially in the national side, and if the way the game was played in England was perfect, there would be no need for change.'

However, according to a *Daily Mirror* poll Ruud was absolutely right to condemn the quality of the Premiership. 61 per cent of readers supported him.

Liam Brady completely backed Gullit by pronouncing that only one man is good enough to become a top star in Italy – Alan Shearer. The former Arsenal and Juventus star said: 'I have to agree with Ruud, there are only a few players who could go over to Italy and set the world alight. But his choices would not be mine. Top of my list would be Shearer. He has the ability to play well anywhere. Sheringham and possibly Ferdinand could do well, but really only Shearer would set the game on fire.' Brady, who also played for Inter Milan, Sampdoria and Ascoli before returning home to West Ham, discounted Gullit's other choices Giggs and Fowler. 'Giggs' style of play would not go down well in Italy ... he runs with the ball and Italian defenders are too good. Fowler hasn't had enough experience in Europe at club or international level.' Brady said history proved just how tough it was in Italy. 'Italy is the toughest place to get goals – Rush, Francis, Hateley and Blissett all went over there and came back because they did not score.'

Gullit was shocked by the generally adverse reaction. For every so-called 'expert' who agreed, there were two or three who didn't. Ruud was amazed by the volume of rage. Usually he would shrug his shoulders and ignore it, this time he felt obliged to put his record straight. Ruud's representative Jon Smith said: 'Ruud is really hurt by all this. There was certainly no insult intended. He gave an interview to an Italian journalist in good faith and has been grossly misrepresented in what he actually said.' Jon Smith's First Artist Management, based at Wembley, had taken on the role as Ruud's advisor and agent a couple of months earlier. Jon and his brother Phil guided Ruud through the most turbulent and distressing episodes. They advised Ruud to issue a statement through the Press Association.

It was hardly the sort of preparation for the FA Cup confrontation with Newcastle United. Ruud endured a spot of backstretching in his quest for fitness ... and a fair bit of ribbing from his team-mates. Gullit didn't hide after training, emerging to stress it had all been a huge misunderstanding. His Chelsea team-mates accepted the explanation and so did Hoddle. Ruud failed to make it for the clash with Newcastle at the Bridge, but he was there for the replay.

Dennis Wise said: 'We were just winding him up about the article in the Italian paper but we accept what he has told us.' Gullit said: 'I was disappointed the way it came out – not embarrassed. It was my intention to give English football a boost.'

Ruud's absence from the short list of six players nominated for the Professional Football Association's Player of the Year award created a great deal of consternation. Les Ferdinand was crowned Player of the Year at a glittering night at the Grosvenor House Hotel in London's Park Lane at the end of March. He had beaten team-mates David Ginola and Peter Beardsley plus Alan Shearer, Robbie Fowler and Steve Stone for the players' votes. Fowler, Liverpool's prolific marksman, was voted Young Player of the Year for the second successive time. The PFA's Premier XI, however, did include Gullit. The full line-up was: David James (Liverpool); Gary Neville (Man Utd), Tony Adams (Arsenal), Ugo Ehiogu (Aston Villa), Alan Wright (Aston Villa); David Ginola (Newcastle), Robert Lee (Newcastle), Steve Stone (Nottingham Forest), Gullit; Les Ferdinand (Newcastle) and Alan Shearer (Blackburn).

Why didn't Gullit make the top six? In fact, why didn't Gullit win it? Neil Harman in the *Daily Mail* wrote: 'Why is it then that only one foreign player, David Ginola of Newcastle is among the six nominees to collect the PFA's Player of the Year award from the greatest of them all, Pele, in London on Sunday night? Could it be there is a residual jealousy among English players that the foreign stars with their magnificent attitude, eloquence on and off the field and intricate love and understanding of football appears largely beyond the levels of English comprehension.'

Brain Glanville observed in his *People* column: 'Perhaps the most significant news last week was that the short-list for the PFA's Player of the Year doesn't include Ruud Gullit. Watching Gullit's magical goal at Stamford Bridge against Manchester City, his glorious display, despite the flu, away to Wimbledon, you marvelled at the sublime amalgam of power and grace, the two complemented by blazing intelligence. And Gullit doesn't make the short list! So just as, according to the French, war is too important to be left to generals, perhaps football is too important to be left to footballers.'

PFA union leader Gordon Taylor puts it down to the timing of the event, rather than to any hidden agenda, such as Ruud's reluctance to join the union. Taylor said: 'The voting takes place principally throughout February, but Ruud seemed to come to prominence far more in the latter stages of the season. It's the same for Cantona. He has made a big impact but only late in the season, particularly as he was suspended until October. And, he didn't get into the top six, either. Yes, it does seem strange that Ruud didn't make the top six, but it's wrong to make such a big thing out of it. We have written to Ruud and Brendon Batson has gone to see him and take his medal to him for winning a place in the Premiership team.'

Taylor rejects the theory that there was a backlash against Gullit for his outspoken comments about the standards of English players. 'I don't think footballers take such views into account, they vote on ability. Certainly there was no ill feeling from within our organisation. If anything we are grateful to Ruud for backing our anti-racist campaign. Personally I am very much aware of the quality he has brought to our game. I was asked to hit out at Gullit's comments about English players, but I resisted because I didn't give it any great substance. I know some people are suggesting that Gullit and Cantona didn't figure as a reaction to the foreign element in our game, but I don't think so.'

There can be little doubt that Ruud's outspoken views about English players reflected to a degree, however, small, in his failure to be nominated for the final list of six players for the PFA awards. Whether he meant it or not, in reality the rest of the world doesn't seem impressed with British players' skills.

It was another painful kick in the pants for our national game when FIFA organised a glittering showpiece match in America on 14th July. The world team picked to face Brazil in the Giants' Stadium, New York, originally didn't contain one English star. There was no room either for the likes of Eric Cantona, David Ginola and Dennis Bergkamp. Yet, Ruud was selected, as the only representative from the Premiership. FIFA were unrepentant in their derisory decision. They pointed out that there hasn't been a world class player from England since the days of Gary Lineker. A FIFA spokesman said: 'This is a world eleven team after all and we have selected representatives from Europe. But when drawing up the 16-strong short list we didn't consider anyone from England as suitable. You don't have a player who is good enough to have captured the imagination of the world or even come to their attention. The last one you had was Gary Lineker but since then no-one has hit our headlines. Your game is very positive in the Premiership of England. And your players seem to have a lot of fun playing their football. But we didn't think anyone was worthy of a call up to represent the world against Brazil.' FIFA, who appointed Danish coach Richard Moller-Nielsen as World XI manager, even 'pinched' Brazilian Romario to make up their numbers. And to cause us further embarrassment they included South African defender Mark Fish, Australian Ned Zelic and even Japanese star Miura in a star studded line up. However, the perception of English talent perked up after Terry Venables' team reached the semi-finals of Euro '96, only to lose to Germany on penalties.

Ruud's charisma was successfully tapped by the BBC as they fought off competition from ITV to snap him up as part of their expert team of studio soccer experts for Euro '96. Gullit, analysing matches as part of the BBC 'team' of Gary Lineker, Alan Hansen and Jimmy Hill, helped earn the corporation the larger slice of the Euro '96 audience, despite the presence on ITV of big names such as Glenn Hoddle, Kevin Keegan, Alex Ferguson and Jack Charlton. 'I've really enjoyed doing it,' he said. 'I'm also very pleased with the response. People have stopped me in the streets and said they like what I say and think I mostly make sense, so that makes me feel good. I take it seriously and I try to make my point clearly.'

His television appearances finally ruled out any thoughts of an international comeback for Gullit. Phil Smith of First Artist Management, Gullit's UK advisers, said: 'He decided some time ago, without malice aforethought, that he'd accomplished what he'd set out to achieve in international football. And then he could concentrate on domestic football. I think he was quite content making the decision at the time and has not seen fit to change it.'

Ruud, who has also appeared on Sky, had been besieged by a variety of media offers. He says: 'I enjoy commentating because you can see the game from a different point of view, you can see what is happening.' Invited on the Sky Sports' *Monday Night Football*, Gullit instantly won over Andy Gray. 'I was impressed with everything about him in the studio. The man is a huge star, but what is nice is how much it comes across that he is enjoying playing and talking about football in England. He takes in all his experiences and logs them cleverly in his head. He's a very deep thinker about the game ... He knows far too much about football, we're not having him on again!'

CHAPTER EIGHT

Ruud Awakening

Millions of people know Ruud Gullit. With Pele, Cruyff and Maradona, his name is known to every little boy playing football on the streets, from Rio de Janeiro to Rome, from New York to Tokyo and London to Moscow. But ask any football fan if they have heard of Rudi Dil, and they would probably shake their head.

On one of Gullit's first trips with the Dutch national side, journalists travelling with the team heard a customs official ask Gullit questions about his passport. The man behind the desk was delighted to recognise the famous Dutchman in the group of professional players passing by at Amsterdam's Schipol airport. But when he happened to take a quick look in Gullit's passport, he saw a photo of a young man without any dreadlocks and with a totally different name. That name was Rudi Dil.

Gullit had to explain that the picture had been taken in his younger days when he was playing football with an 'Ian Wright-style' haircut and that Ruud Gullit was the name he used as a footballer. The puzzled journalists in the queue behind were both amused and amazed. But it revealed something nobody had ever known in the career of Ruud Gullit.

The name Rudi Dil comes from his Dutch mother, Ria Dil. For

personal reasons she wanted him to be registered and named, at his birth on 1st September 1962, after her and not his father, George Gullit, who was born in Surinam, a former Dutch colony, near the Caribbean in South America.

When Rudi Dil was thriteen, he knew he was going to be a professional footballer one day but he thought the name 'Dil' did not sound right. So he told people they had to call him Gullit, after his dad. And not Rudi, but Ruud. The player has never admitted or revealed whether the real reason behind the name change was that he wanted to have his father's name, like every other boy or girl in his class.

George Gullit and Ria Dil met in Holland. George was a former international footballer for his country, Surinam, and took a university degree course in economics in Holland. He was teaching economics at a high school, but decided to go back to his home country after he became unemployed and the relationship with Ruud Gullit's mother had ended. George Gullit returned in 1985, when Ruud was already a professional.

George is now sixty-one and lives in Paramaribo, the capital of Surinam. He trains the youth team of local club Santos and has retired from his job. George Gullit spent twenty years with his son and was heavily involved in his career. He recognised at a very early stage that his only boy had a fabulous football talent. Like every father, he was proud of his son and would tell people in the street that Ruud would play for the national team one day. Ruud was indeed a brilliant footballer both in the street and for his local amateur club, Meerboys. So no one laughed at George Gullit, and they took all his proud claims very seriously. They, too, could see that this boy was special.

George Gullit, himself, played in the first teams of Real Sranang, Sonny Boys and Transvaal in the top league of Surinam. If people wonder where Ruud gets his phenomenal shooting power from, they only have to look at his father's muscular legs. At Real Sranang, and later in other Surinam sides, George played alongside a man who was his best friend and who was to proudly boast of a famous son too – he was the father of Frank Rijkaard. Together they moved to Holland and found accommodation in the same area, the 'Jordaan', Amsterdam's oldest district and the Jewish quarter. In the middle of the city the Jordaan is a most colourful area. It is not a coincidence that most of the famous Dutch actors, singers or film stars have come from the Jordaan. It was, and still is, a place where life starts from scratch and where people socialise in the streets.

It is a miraculous story that two little boys, future international team-mates for Holland, with Amsterdam-born mothers and Surinam-born fathers, grew up at the same time in the same area. Ruud Gullit and Frank Rijkaard were playing football in the street when they were six years old. Some 20 years later, still together, they lifted European Cups and international trophies.

George Gullit was not a bad player himself, but he knows, and admits, that his talents are only four or five per cent that of his son's. 'The only resemblance I can see is the shooting power,' says George. 'I used to take all the free kicks in the teams I played for. Defenders were shaking as they formed the wall in front of goal. My shooting ability was probably my biggest asset as a player. That's why it is not a surprise that Ruud has scored so many fabulous goals from free kicks all through his career.'

At the end of the 1960s it was not possible for school boys to play football for a team under the age of eight. However, when his son was seven years old, George knew that it was almost impossible to keep him away from a football pitch any longer. Ruud was a very strong, well-built boy. He was bigger than all his friends of the same age, but more important was his ability to take on even bigger boys in a football match. So Ruud was delighted when the board of local club FC Meerboys registered him as an official youth player at the age of seven.

He stayed with Meerboys for six years. His first coach, Jan Terreehorst, now seventy-two, still remembers the days when people stood watching with complete astonishment at how one, dark looking boy would score all the goals in every match. Sometimes five, sometimes eight. Like Ruud's father, Terreehorst tried to explain to the wonder kid that football was a team sport and that he had to try and pass the ball to other players, too! 'But Ruud did not see any other players. He just picked the ball up from his own goalkeeper, went past every opponent he met on the way to the goal on the other side of the pitch, and put the ball in the net.'

In a desperate effort to stop him from keeping the ball to himself all the time, Jan Terreehorst told the young Gullit that he was not allowed to go any further with the ball than the half-way line. Terreehorst recalls: 'You know what he did then? He ran up to the half-way line and then hit the ball from there. It still finished in the net! He was 11 years old and could score from the half-way line! I remembered being thrilled to bits when he did that. But of course, it still was not nice for the other kids. So, after the match we told him off!'

George says, 'I even tried to punish him by letting him walk home after matches. Instead of cycling home or taking the bus, I would let him walk all the way. I said to him, if he could do everything on his own during a football match, then he could also make his own way home afterwards. But it did not bother him. He would run all the way and arrive at the front door before me!'

Most of Gullit's friends at school were playing for Ajax, the biggest and most prestigious club in Amsterdam. Ajax has a huge reputation in football. They produce wonderful talent, but Ruud did not even want to talk about going to Ajax. With his best friend

Frank Rijkaard, he only wanted to go to DWS, a non-league club with a very good youth policy at the time.

Many scouts of professional clubs looked at the talented players at DWS. Among them was a British coach, Barry Hughes, who had played with Don Howe and Bobby Robson at West Bromwich Albion. Hughes finished his career in Holland and stayed there after he married Dutch television celebrity Elles Berger. He then went into football management and was boss of FC Haarlem, a First Division club 20 miles from Amsterdam. As Haarlem did not have the financial resources to buy big name players on the transfer market, Barry had to try and discover players at amateur level.

At DWS, Frank Rijkaard's name was already in every scout's notebook. Of course, Barry thought the young Rijkaard was a brilliant, skilful player. But unlike all the other scouts and coaches who used to pay visits to the youth teams of DWS, Barry was struck by another player in the team. Hughes thought his pace, his ability to score from great distances with both feet, his flair and his leadership were incredible for a young boy. His name was Ruud Gullit.

Hughes says, 'I was mesmerized in the first year I saw him. I just kept wanting to watch this kid. Frank Rijkaard was a lovely player to watch, too. I had known him for quite a while. I knew his dad because I had played with him at Blauw Wit. But for some reason I could not take my eyes of Ruud Gullit. When he was 15 years old, I decided to approach the boy. After a game I went up to him and asked him if he fancied a move to FC Haarlem.

'Ruud told me that I would have to speak to his dad about that. He pointed out who his dad was, so I went up to him. Ruud just strolled off and went to have a shower. George Gullit thought it was too early for a move to Haarlem. Ruud, at the time, was not doing all that well at school. His mind was more on football than on homework, and George insisted that Ruud should pass a couple of 'O' levels before trying to become a professional footballer.

'So Ruud's dad asked me to come back a year later. Well, determined to get this boy as I was, I said: 'Well, Mr Gullit, you'd better write that date in your diary, because I will be on your doorstep.' That did impress them, because exactly a year later, on the same day, at the same hour, I knocked on their door.'

Many years later, Ruud revealed that Barry had stunned both him and his dad with that attitude. Gullit said: 'Barry Hughes did indeed show how much he wanted to sign me and how he was trying to get the best for his club. It was the main reason why I liked this man and why I wanted to play for him, rather than for Ajax or Belgian champions Anderlecht who had showed an interest too.' Anderlecht had even offered the Gullit family a car to use between Brussels and Amsterdam, as well as £35,000. But paramount to George, was his son passing his exams.

Barry Hughes recalls: 'When I was negotiating with George Gullit, Ruud was sitting in the room and listening to everything that was said. George pointed it out, once more to me, that school exams at the end of the season were more important than goals or contracts. So I promised to find him an excellent school in Haarlem and offer him a bonus in his contract of £500 if he passed his exams. It helped. George and Ruud Gullit signed for FC Haarlem and I was the happiest man in the world.'

On Sunday 19th August 1979, Ruud Gullit made his debut as the youngest player ever in Dutch professional football. The 16-year-old was centre-half in the Haarlem defence and came through his first match very well. Despite the quality Ruud added to the side, FC Haarlem did not stay in the First Division that season. The club once again had been punished for selling its best players.

But a year later Gullit bounced back with Haarlem. He was no longer a defender, but was playing as a central striker and scored 14 goals that season. Haarlem were crowned champions of the Second Division and were back at the highest level within 12 months. Gullit was voted the Second Division's Player of the Year by his fellow pros and the media. He received the Silver Boot, his first personal trophy.

It was during this time that the first of several English clubs became interested in Gullit. Arsenal manager, Terry Neill and coach Don Howe came over to watch the 17-year-old play for Haarlem but flew home unimpressed. Howe's old West Bromwich team-mate Barry Hughes said: 'I begged them to take another look, but I heard nothing more for a couple of years. Then Don rang and said 'You were right about him!' Everyone drops a clanger somewhere along the line, so I'm not blaming Don for his. But I bet it still hurts.' Hughes had given the Highbury hierarchy the invitation to watch the kid he had groomed from a 15-year-old. Hughes said: 'The first time I saw him I knew I had found the Dutch Duncan Edwards.'

Gullit was soccer-mad and knew more about Arsenal than the average fan. Hughes adds: 'I'd told Ruud so much about English football the lad was dreaming of wearing the red shirt of Arsenal. He could see himself in the marble halls. Don and Terry came to Holland to see him play and he was theirs for the taking. I asked them for £200,000 but we were so short of money I would have accepted £80,000. Ruud didn't have the best of games, but I asked them to rely on my opinion and take him anyway. I'd have taken him like a shot because, although he was only 17, he had everything he has today. The only difference is that he's older, bigger and stronger.'

In his third season in professional football, Gullit finished fourth with Haarlem in the First Division. It meant that Haarlem qualified for Europe the following season, although Ruud was destined not be part of the team that competed in the UEFA Cup tournament. In April 1982, at the age of 18, he signed a three year contract with Feyenoord, the Rotterdam club paying £300,000 to Haarlem. With Gullit's departure, FC Haarlem lost its last famous player. The club has never been able to get over that loss and has since struggled at the bottom of the Second Division.

Despite having to concentrate heavily on his football career, Gullit still had an eye for other facets in life too. Asked what was the most disappointing thing in 1983, Gullit said, 'The growing fascism in Europe. I read a number of articles about the young fascists in certain countries. I also saw a documentary on television. It frightened me.'

That year Gullit was asked to open an international exhibition in the Anne Frank House in Amsterdam, a Dutch Jewish museum. Gullit supported it strongly because it helped young people to think about the effects of violence and racism in society. His opinion had been influenced by a number of incidents in that football season. On the 14th September 1983, Ruud played his first European Cup game for Feyenoord. In the UEFA Cup first round, they had drawn St Mirren, with an away match in Scotland for the first time.

Gullit was the only black player in the Feyenoord team and one of the first black players to play in Scotland. He was the best player on the pitch, he scored the only goal and was impressive as ever. But to his own surprise and the whole of the Feyenoord team, the Scottish fans booed and taunted him for 90 minutes.

Feyenoord director Fred Blankemeyer recalls: 'He was brilliant. I think it was one of the best matches he ever played for us. But the things that were shouted at him from the stands by the Scottish supporters were awful. He did not show it, but I knew he was hurt. They were making 'jungle noises', they were imitating monkeys, they booed and whistled even if he came near the ball. We thought it was disgusting. I am sure it left a big scar with him.'

Gullit later described that night at St Mirren as one of the worst things that happened to him in football. But another incident, not concerning himself, was described by Gullit as just as appalling.

After beating St Mirren, Feyenoord had to play Tottenham Hotspur in the second round of the UEFA Cup. It was the first time he met Glenn Hoddle. Tottenham had a marvellous side at that time, with Hoddle even outshining Johan Cruyff and the young Gullit. At White Hart Lane, in the first leg, Tottenham beat Feyenoord 4–2.

In the return match the Feyenoord stadium was packed to capacity with 50,000 people. Thousands of Tottenham fans had travelled to Holland and before the game hooligans from Feyenoord and Spurs clashed in the stands. Knives were pulled and more than a dozen fans were injured.

Gullit was shocked when he saw all the fighting in the crowd. He played on the right flank of the Feyenoord team, in front of the stand, where in the first half, all the trouble had occurred. Feyenoord lost the game again, 2–0. But the off the field incidents had bothered Gullit more than the defeat.

Gullit said: 'You know what shocked me most of all? The pictures I saw in a newspaper of Adolf Hitler on the wall in the bedroom of this young lad who stabbed a Tottenham Hotspur fan. I thought it was shocking and sickening. Since then, I have followed everything on this subject. The only thing that worries me is that we, as a nation, have got little power to do anything about it.'

In 1984 Gullit won his first major trophy when Feyenoord lifted the League Championship. Also in the side at the time was one of the world's all-time greats – Johan Cruyff. The Dutch maestro had only joined Feyenoord for one season and was to retire from professional football after that. Cruyff's contract with Feyenoord had surprised the whole nation, as he had grown up in Amsterdam and played for Ajax for most of his career. But a feud with his old club, after his long spell with Barcelona, made Cruyff go to Feyenoord. In Rotterdam he could fulfil his revenge on Ajax by showing them he was still fit enough to play at the highest level. The board of Ajax had told him they had doubts about his fitness and his influence on other players at the club.

Gullit had welcomed Cruyff at Feyenoord. As a young player he felt as if he could not wish for anyone better alongside him to learn everything about the game, 'I really think it was wonderful to have two of the most influential players in the history of Dutch football at Feyenoord when I played there. Johan Cruyff was one of them, Wim van Hanegem was the other. Van Hanegem and Cruyff were the two big names in the Dutch national team in 1974, when Holland reached the final of the World Cup.

'Van Hanegem had just retired but got a job as assistant manager at the club. He was training with us every day and was a marvellous man to work with. He became one of the most important people in my life. Not only because of the game, but because I could turn to him if I wanted a chat or if I needed somebody to talk to. I used to visit his house and talk to him for hours. After leaving Feyenoord, I always kept in touch with him. When we see each other now, the relationship is still good.'

With Cruyff, Gullit had a different understanding. It was just as good as with Van Hanegem, but more concentrated on football. 'Johan knew everything about the game. He was a perfectionist. It was a delight to train with him every day, to play with him in every match. I think I was really lucky. Who has had Johan Cruyff as a tutor in his early days? The funny thing was that Cruyff did not only pass on his expertise about football, but about almost everything in sport. It used to make me laugh so much. He claimed he knew everything. If two players were having a game of snooker, he would stop the game and pick up one of the cues. He would ask them why they were taking a shot like that and would tell them it would be better to play the ball different. Honestly, he really used to crack me up.

'But I have always had the biggest possible respect for him, as nobody must forget he was one of the best players in the world and later turned out to be one of the best coaches in the world. It was not just the name of Johan Cruyff we wanted for the national team, it was his tactical knowledge, his experience, really everything about the man.'

Unfortunately for Gullit it never happened. Several times Gullit tried to convince the Dutch FA that Johan Cruyff was an ideal candidate for the job. But like the English FA, who never took on Brian Clough, the Dutch were frightened Cruyff would turn the headquarters of the their FA upside down.

When Gullit moved to Feyenoord his wages soared to £100,000 a year from the £40,000 he was earning at FC Haarlem. At Feyenoord he became the club's highest paid player but he was alerted by two of his team-mates, Peter Houtman and Wim van Hanegem that he could make a fortune off the pitch, if he joined them in a company called Fast Play Ltd. He eagerly did so.

The three players had one agent, Nico de Raadt, and he made all their appointments and conducted all deals. Fast Play organised football camps in the summer, where Gullit and the other players taught youngsters their skills and how to be better players. But very soon, de Raadt realised that Gullit was dominating the company. De Raadt recalls, 'Already in his first year at Feyenoord, Ruud Gullit had such an impact that everybody wanted to do commercial things with him. They were not interested in anybody else, they only wanted Gullit. If somebody wanted to open a shop, Ruud turned up and within 20 minutes there were thousands packed in the high street of the town where the shop was situated.

'I knew we could go into bigger deals very quickly. His first major TV advert made him £20,000. All he had to do was tell the public how much he enjoyed reading the *Algemeen Dagblad* morning paper every day.'

His public appearances off the pitch were just as impressive as his displays on it, as businessmen and companies soon discovered. In his days at Feyenoord, he would charge £400 for opening a new shop. He considered that sum, at the time, a lot of money for half an hour's work ... but in the years that followed he was going to earn 100 times that amount for even less effort.

He attracted huge offers from sports manufactures Adidas and Lotto. By the time he signed for PSV Eindhoven in 1985, where he earned £350,000 a year for playing 48 matches, he made more money through commercial activities than he did as a player. Nico de Raadt says, 'In his first year, we already had a turnover of more than one million guilders.'

At PSV, the fans and players were very excited when Gullit was bought from Feyenoord, for the club had at last signed a world-class star. Gullit indeed emerged as a fantastic footballer. He played in the sweeper role, often joining the attack and penetrating deeply into the heart of the opposing team's half. Gullit scored an amazing 24 goals in his first season – a new world record for a defender. His contribution was a significant factor in PSV winning the League Championship that season.

Just as thrilled as the fans were the chief executives of Philips, the electronics giant who owned PSV. They realised that Ruud Gullit could be the best 'salesman' they had in the entire company. They asked him to do commercials for the club, presenting the new Philips iron or the latest electric shaver. Gullit co-operated to please his employers. However, it wasn't long before their relationship turned sour. In 1987, the Italian club AC Milan wanted to buy Gullit, but PSV refused to sell their star player. Gullit launched a bitter attack on the people in charge of PSV and Philips. In an interview in a weekly Dutch magazine, he strongly accused the club of lacking flair, claiming they would never get the same response abroad as Ajax and Feyenoord.

'I have tried everything to help this club. I have even told them that we had the wrong tactics in the team. We were not going anywhere. I have written letters to our manager, Hans Kraay, suggesting different line-ups. I have proposed to play striker, to play behind the front two, to play sweeper or on the wing ... anywhere to change things on the pitch. I did not get a reply. That is why I feel I am being blocked in my development. I want to achieve more things than PSV do. I am more ambitious than the club.'

PSV had slipped in the league that season and were not playing as well as the year before. Ruud was the only player who seemed to be in great form. He said: 'PSV think they can just use me like a little kid. Because they don't know how to play, they keep putting me in different positions during the match. When we are 1–0 down, they put me up front to sort out that end and to score goals. When we are winning, I am directed to the back four again.

'The board members of Philips are acting no differently. If a new Philips mixer or hoover is not selling well, they call me and I have to advertise with these things in a full colour brochure or leaflet. Look at the things they sell, you can find me on almost every page of their brochures. Sometimes I think I *look* like a hoover or an iron.'

The management of PSV Eindhoven was shocked. Hans Kraay, in charge of the first team, insisted that Gullit should be heavily fined or even sacked. Kraay said: 'A player who talks so low about the club who pay him such a big salary every year, does not deserve to play for PSV any longer. I can't accept his accusations. Gullit will be banned for the rest of the season. He can go and sit in the stand and watch the team play without him.'

But of course, PSV could not afford to lose Ruud Gullit. They needed him badly. So, after one of the most hectic weeks in the history of PSV Eindhoven, it was not Gullit who was sacked, but manager Hans Kraay.

PSV, however, realised that they had a very unhappy employee and decided to re-open negotiations with Silvio Berlusconi of AC Milan, who had already told them that he wanted to buy Gullit. On 21 March 1987 both clubs agreed a fee of £5.5 million – a world record at that time – and Gullit was on his way to Italy.

CHAPTER NINE

Italy – the Dream that Turned Sour

Wherever Ruud Gullit goes he is a catalyst for change. He says he is always looking for a fresh challenge: 'If you look at my career you will see that I have always signed for clubs where I can create something. I never wanted to go to a club where everything was laid out for me, where all the trophies were already in the silver room and where there was complete satisfaction. I can't see the challenge there, I can't see any fun when the sheets are spread in the bed, as the Dutch would say.

'AC Milan are a big club now, but everybody forgets that they were almost bankrupt in 1986 when Silvio Berlusconi came to the rescue. I joined them in 1987 and the rest is well known. At AC Milan I tried to help build a team which was strong enough to win everything in the game. It was probably the best team I have ever played for.'

Gullit did more than anyone to transform Milan from a mediocre outfit to one of the greatest forces in European football. In his first year in Italy he was voted Best New Foreign Player in *Serie A*. However, the major prize that season was the League Championship – Milan's first league success for a decade.

His first few matches for AC Milan were breathtaking and the crowd in the San Siro stadium were immediately won over by Ruud. He made an impact with some astonishing free-kicks, saying at the time: 'It's not only Ronald Koeman who can kick a ball from long distance. The hard work, which I have put in at training, is paying off now. Every day, when training is finished, I put up a wall made from wooden puppets and I practise for more than thirty minutes.

'You see, in Italy you have to specialise in free-kicks, as you don't get many chances in a match. Every dead moment is vital. When I take free-kicks, I don't try and copy Michel Platini. I usually look at Virdis in our own team. He is brilliant at curling a ball into the top corner.'

In October 1987, when he returned to Holland for an international game, he told the Dutch media how he was surprised it had only taken him a short time to fit into Italian football. He said: 'It was not the life off the pitch, which I was dreading, as most footballers do when they go abroad. It was the football itself, which I thought might be hard to get used to. But it has all gone extremely well, I have enjoyed every minute of my first few months in Milan.

'One of the most peculiar things is that we stay in hotels so much. I don't mind that. It is good to concentrate on your job properly. It has brought me into a routine of spending most of the nights of the week in a hotel. If we play at home we go into a hotel on the Saturday. If we play away, we leave two or three days before the match. When I get home, I unpack my bags and I get my stuff ready for the next game.

'Mr Berlusconi visits our training complex, Milanello, regularly. He comes into the dressing room before every match, too. But he does not get involved in team tactics. He leaves everything to the manager and the professionals. However, Berlusconi always wants us to represent the club in the proper way. I talk to the press almost every day, but I hardly read the newspapers the following morning. I can't be bothered. The amount of stories which are published about me every day, is incredible.'

Gullit dismissed comments made at the time by the Dutch national coach Rinus Michels who said the standard of Italian football was poor. Ruud said: 'Michels should never have compared Dutch football with the Italian game. In Holland there are only two or three big clubs. In Italy every team is capable of beating any other side in the league. It makes people think about tactics and stops coaches from attacking like mad. You have to be sensible and clever if you want to survive in *Serie A*.'

Gullit's position for most of the his first season at AC Milan was the right wing. With the Dutch national team he had a different role, mostly in midfield. But Milan coach Arrigo Sacchi thought Ruud was at his best out wide. Gullit did not argue: 'I never complained in my first season about the position. Sacchi tried me as a midfield player in the beginning, but he thought I was better as an attacker. People have been discussing for years where I should play and where I fit in best. But nobody asks me! Well, in fact, I don't mind where I play, as long as they don't mess me about. I don't want to be playing in one position this week and in another the next. If they start shifting me every time we lose, I get irritable.'

His contribution to the championship triumph of AC Milan was enormous. Ruud was the key factor in the team, the man who could motivate other players and bring the best out of his team-mates. The people of Milan went absolutely crazy about the success Gullit helped bring to the club. He had a glorious first year – playing 29 games out of 34, scoring nine goals.

The league title was clinched two games before the end of the season against Napoli. Ruud had a fantastic match but still stayed down to earth: 'We celebrated in style, nothing over the top. We had to play Juventus in the next match. It goes with the professional attitude of the players, which I found very high in Italy.'

The 1987–88 season was also the first year Ruud played alongside Marco van Basten at club level. The two 'giants' in Dutch football got on extremely well. In the van Basten biography, *His Life, His Work*, Gullit talks about the perfect understanding they had on and off the pitch.

'I do enjoy playing with Marco van Basten. We get on really well in the front line. He is an out and out striker. I try to serve him from the wing. It works very well. But it's true, when we play for Holland I am behind him, instead of next to him.

'The best thing about having Marco in your team, and as a friend, is that nothing in the world can put him off. He has an incredible mental strength. No matter how much people criticise him, he just does not get worked up. He might say: 'Sod them'. And that will be it. I think that is great. He just gets on with life and his own job.'

Ruud rated Marco van Basten, in his first year at AC Milan, as one of the best strikers in the world. He soon noticed the fabulous goalscoring instinct of the forward, even in the tough *Serie A*. Ruud said: 'He could do things on one square yard of grass, which other players can't even dream of. But I could never be jealous of him. I don't think Marco will ever be jealous either. We do like winning trophies, including personal honours like the European or World Player of the Year awards. But if I win it, he is happy for me. If he wins it, I will be over the moon for Marco.'

In his second season things just carried on where they had stopped the year before. Ruud played 28 league matches and scored 11 league goals and further success came to Milan – this time in Europe. At the beginning of the season Ruud's old mate Frank Rijkaard joined him and Marco van Basten, and the three Dutch superstars gave AC Milan an invincible character. The climax of the Dutch influence at the club would come in the European Cup Final against Steaua Bucharest in Barcelona's Nou Camp stadium.

The Final was dominated by AC Milan. After 18 minutes Ruud scored a marvellous goal. Ten minutes later van Basten made it 2–0 and before half-time, Ruud had scored AC Milan's third goal. Just after the break van Basten made it 4–0.

It was a remarkable performance for Gullit who was not fully fit at the time. In the semi-final against Real Madrid, five weeks before, he had been carried off with a cartilage injury which had required surgery. But he returned for the Final and had an outstanding game. Not only did he score twice, but he hit the post and was a constant threat to the Romanian side. He was substituted after 59 minutes, with the game already won, and left the field to a standing ovation from the crowd.

AC Milan's domination of the European game was highly rated by the football experts in Europe. Milan were suddenly among the television stars of Berlusconi's electronic empire and he had even flown in his own TV crews and equipment to Barcelona for the Final when the Spanish technicians went on strike. His investment was well rewarded with Milan's sweeping victory.

Gullit said that European Cup win was the highlight of his great career: 'The whole stadium was red and white. My Milan side played so well, it gave me great satisfaction. I also enjoyed my first championship in the Italian league which no one expected us to win. I was playing against Diego Maradona but no one thought we would take the title away from his Napoli side. It was such a pleasure to be part of that Milan team, they had a different kind of style, a different mentality towards the game. It was a highly successful cocktail of the Dutch influence, players who didn't care and who just wanted to attack, and the Italian approach of not giving anything away. The mixture was formidable. We were six years ahead of our time.'

In December 1989 Milan went to Tokyo to play South American champions Atletico Nacional of Columbia. They picked up another major trophy by winning the World Club Championship, 1–0, with Evani scoring the winner in extra-time.

With Gullit now established as one of the world's top players he was well rewarded by his club. At AC Milan he earned £20,000 a week. He signed a three-year contract and now had a new agent. Nico de Raadt had been a good agent for him in Holland, but when he moved to AC Milan he needed a more experienced negotiator. That was Cor Coster, the father-in-law of Johan Cruyff.

Cor Coster was the partner of Apollonius Konijnenburg who had a company called Interpro. They were charging their clients (Gullit, Van Basten, Rijkaard) the same fees as accountants or lawyers. For every major commercial contract they claimed 30 per cent. Cor Coster said he thought that was a very reasonable fee: 'For both Ruud Gullit and Marco van Basten I got fabulous boot deals. Ruud Gullit's contract with Lotto earned him £400,000. Marco van Basten's first contract with Diadora earned him £350,000. I don't think they mind that I have a provision in such a big contract.'

Coster and Konijnenburg turned Ruud Gullit into a huge industry. They made sure Gullit was earning astonishing figures from all his commercial deals and other appearances. Television, newspaper interviews, hats, scarves, wigs (with dreadlocks), quilt covers, video tapes, anything you could think of, had Gullit's face or name on it and sold out!

In Gullit's third year in Italy everything suddenly turned a little sour when he was sidelined most of the time with knee injuries. He only started two league games and scored just one goal.

However, he was to play a major role that season despite his crippling injuries. AC Milan won the European Cup with Gullit making a surprising appearance in the Final.

In the early stages of the competition, the injured Gullit was a big miss to AC Milan who struggled to recapture their brilliant form of the previous season. They failed to dominate the European ties as they had done before. They disposed of HJK Helsinki in the first round 5–0 overall, but squeezed past Real Madrid 2–1 in the second round. Milan needed extra-time against KV Mechelen (Belgium) in the quarter-finals and Bayern Munich in the semis.

In the Final they faced Benfica and Gullit was a shock inclusion in the AC Milan side. He had just come back from another major operation and Ruud admitted after the game: 'All Sacchi wanted from me was that I was present on the pitch. Really, that was all!'

Sacchi knew that their opponents, who were not aware of Gullit's physical problems, would change all their tactics if the Dutchman was in the side, and concentrate on defending more than attacking. Like almost every other team, Benfica were frightened by the name of Ruud Gullit. The tactics worked with AC Milan again clinching the European Cup with a single goal from Frank Rijkaard.

After all his operations and the disappointing World Cup in Italy, Ruud came back strongly for the team in 1990. However, for the first time since he had joined the club they did not win a domestic or European trophy. Although, Milan did win the World Club Championship again. In Tokyo they beat Olimpia Ascuncion of Paraguay, the new South American Champions. Milan won 3–0, with two goals from Frank Rijkaard and one from Stroppa.

But there was to be disappointment in the European Cup. Milan entered the competition at the second round after receiving a bye. They faced the Belgian champions Brugge, and were held to a goalless draw in the San Siro stadium. Away in Belgium, they made up for their poor performance two weeks earlier and beat Brugge 1–0.

It was a clear sign that not everything was going smoothly for AC Milan. In the quarter-finals they had to face Bernard Tapie's Olympique Marseille. It was a clash of two tycoons, as Tapie and Berlusconi had both invested millions in their sides. In the home tie, Gullit scored in front of 83,000 people after 14 minutes. But his goal was not enough for Milan. Marseille's Jean-Pierre Papin equalised before half-time and the game ended 1–1. Milan were without Marco van Basten who was suspended for both matches in the tie.

Ruud knew they were facing a difficult job. In Marseille the French were going crazy about the possibility of knocking out the reigning European and World Champions. What followed was one of the most bizarre European games ever played. In front of a 38,000 capacity crowd in Marseille, Milan struggled again. Chris Waddle set the stadium alight when he fired home the only goal of the game fifteen minutes from the end. Milan's fantastic run in Europe seemed to be coming to an end and it all looked very dark for the Italians. On the pitch it looked even darker, as near the end of the match some of the floodlights went out. The Milan team left the field and refused to come back on to the pitch. After a long break the Swedish referee decided the game should continue but Milan would not return to the field. The match was abandoned and the Cup-holders went out of the Champions Cup in disgrace. UEFA later took strong sanctions. They changed the result into a 3–0 victory for Marseille and suspended Milan for one season from taking part in any European Cup competition.

Gullit's dream move to Italian football was beginning to turn sour and things got worse in the summer of 1991. There was an 'anti-Gullit' group within the club with some directors having doubts about his fitness for the new season. They had bought Jean-Pierre Papin and the Yugoslav Boban. Papin was supposed to be the back-up for Gullit and at the time the Frenchman said he would agree to be on the bench for Gullit, who could pick his matches and have a rest when he liked. But of course it did not work like that. Papin had just been voted European Footballer of the Year and Gullit was far too ambitious to make way for Papin on a voluntary basis.

By September Gullit was fed up with the situation at AC Milan, who by then had six foreigners under contract. In the media there was a big debate about who should play and who should not. Some Italian journalists were used by the directors of AC Milan. Gullit felt people were betraying him and playing 'dirty games'. It all resulted in Gullit getting into his car after a training session and driving straight to Silvio Berlusconi's office one morning. He stormed into the room and demanded to have a meeting with the media-tycoon immediately. Berlusconi turned up within a couple of minutes, which showed what power Gullit has as a player. For any other player the doors would probably have stayed shut.

Gullit asked Berlusconi one simple question. 'Do you want me at AC Milan or not?' Berlusconi was flabbergasted. He was also disappointed, as he made it clear that Gullit, for him, was the big star of his team. He had no doubts about him and if he wanted to he could renew his contract and sign for another three years. Berlusconi even said there would be a job for life within the club for Gullit. It was all Ruud needed to hear. He did not want to discuss the matter with the coach, nor with any other director or commercial manager. If Gullit had a problem, he went straight to Berlusconi.

His first troubles at Milan, however, led to renewed interest from other clubs. In 1991 he had another year of his contract to run at AC Milan, but interested managers were ringing his agent Cor Coster all the time. Cor Coster gave his view of Gullit's problems at AC Milan: 'Ruud is a player with a lot of pride. He is a very sensitive and emotional person too. If he feels people have hurt him or tried to damage his career, he will make sure he gets his own back on them. He has incredible will power. He will not let anybody beat him. He will always hit back at his critics. If people write bad things about him, he will score a fabulous goal in his next match or perform outstandingly.'

Marco van Basten says Ruud's career is like every major sportsman – full of highlights, success, controversy and disappointments. 'First there was the incredible speed, which brought him more or less to top of the world. Then there was all the success with the Dutch national team, with AC Milan in *Serie A* and in Europe for many years. Finally, there were the injuries and his problems in his private life. One thing I could never understand about Gullit was why he sometimes felt threatened. When AC Milan bought Jean-Pierre Papin I should have felt more under pressure than Ruud. But he took it like an insult.'

When Fabio Capello was appointed as the new coach at AC Milan, Gullit was to find himself in and out of the side. Ruud did not get on with Capello. Arrigo Sacchi had been a wonderful manager, with whom he could talk to for hours. But he had little understanding with the new coach. Under Sacchi he had had so much more joy and pleasure. Even if all he could do was stand up straight and kick the ball, Sacchi would play him.

In his last season with AC Milan Gullit spent much of his time watching from the stand instead of playing. Capello believed Gullit's knee was not strong enough to play every week. In the end he only played fifteen league matches. Gullit was determined to prove his manager wrong at a new club. 'I had had enough. I still scored seven goals in those fifteen matches. But I could not cope with Capello's decisions any longer. He did not explain anything to me. One day I turned up for an away match. As I waited to get on the coach, Capello asked me what I was doing. I was not even on the team list. 'Did I not tell you that you can have a couple of days off?' Capello said to me.'

No other manager had ever humiliated Gullit so much. The fact that all his colleagues stood there and watched it happen, made things even worse. Another humiliation was the fact that Capello made Gullit fight for a place on the bench with Jean-Pierre Papin for the European Cup Final in 1993 against Marseille. Papin won and Gullit had to watch the match from the sidelines. Gullit said: 'I was not a hundred percent fit, but I could have come on in the second half if the team had needed me. In the end it was frustrating to train under Capello. I did not know what I was training for.'

AC Milan lost the Final against Olympique Marseille 1–0. The fact that he was left out of the side was to be the last straw for Gullit and he decided to leave Milan. When this was made public, clubs queued up. Olympique Marseille, Paris Saint Germain, Torino, Athletico Madrid, Bayern Munich, four Japanese clubs; everyone wanted him. At the time of this speculation, Ruud had to cancel an appointment with Nelson Mandela, who had not long been released from jail. Gullit said: 'I was just as much disappointed as Mandela. But I had to make very important decisions about my future. I was talking to several clubs and I could not just walk out of the negotiations to fly to South Africa.'

Bayern Munich thought they had won the race for Gullit's signature. Bayern director Franz Beckenbauer flew by private plane to Italy. They had dinner at an exclusive restaurant outside Milan and then Beckenbauer flew over to see Gullit's Dutch solicitor in Amsterdam a couple of days later. The media followed every move. But at the last minute Gullit did a complete turnaround and decided to sign for Italian club Sampdoria, who had joined the chasing clubs at a late stage.

Most of the newspapers hinted that Gullit's new Italian wife did not want to move to Germany, but the player categorically denied that. 'I will keep the real reason to myself. Whatever reason, a player of my status gives, it would be taken as an insult to the Germans. You can imagine what would have happened in Germany, if I had said that I was afraid of racism in the Bundesliga if I go and play there. That would definitely have been a big insult to the Germans. It doesn't bother me that rumours about my wife started. Only I know the truth.'

Gullit decided on Sampdoria, because more than any other club they were known throughout Italy for their friendly atmosphere. The players at Sampdoria once swore in a local pizzeria that nobody would quit the club until they had won a major trophy. President Paolo Mantovai looked upon Sampdoria as one big family, living in harmony. Gullit remembers the day that he walked into the dressing room. 'They had not given me a number yet. They asked me which number I wanted. 'Give me number 4. I have never played with number 4 yet.' They all laughed and so did I. None of the players made any objections. I just put on the shirt and played up front for a whole season with number 4 on my back.'

Ruud enjoyed life in Genoa with Sampdoria. 'They are not on the front page of the newspapers every day. When I was with AC Milan I sometimes hated my own name. A week could not go by when I was not on the front page of the Italian newspapers. At Milanello, the training complex of AC Milan, 15 to 20 reporters turned up every day. And we could not always say 'no'. Some things we had to do: like giving interviews to reporters who were working for Berlusconi's television companies. I did not like going on talk shows either. You see, if you are on the front page every day and with your face on television every other day, people get fed up with you. They will say, oh dear, it's Gullit again.'

At Sampdoria things were more relaxed. The night before a game the team stayed at the same hotel in Nervi. If the wives wanted to pay a visit to their husbands, they could. It was in sharp contrast to AC Milan. 'That was a prison. I hated it. We went into hibernation for 48 hours before every match.'

Gullit enjoyed his time at Sampdoria. After his much publicised and forced departure from AC Milan, Ruud wanted to show Italy he was far from out of place at the highest level of club football in Europe, the *Serie A*.

In 1993 he made a whole new start to his career, leaving his biggest critics amazed. When Ruud had first gone to Italy, he made a glittering start for AC Milan, scoring six goals in six weeks and producing very impressive performances. With Sampdoria he repeated that feat at the beginning of the 1993–94 season. In October 1993 his terrific form made him top scorer in *Serie A* – for the second time in his Italian spell. Gullit-mania broke out. This time in Genoa, where the fans and the media loved him more than any other star in sport or showbusiness.

In the last weekend of October, Gullit had to play his old club AC Milan in a league match. The week before the match, he was asked by every journalist in Italy if he was set to seek revenge on his old club. On the Friday before the game Gullit got frustrated with those questions and snapped at one of the reporters: 'Shut up with your ridiculous stories. Revenge? Me? You should all know me better by now. I would like to show I am still fit and I still enjoy football at the highest level.

'But revenge is something I don't know anything about, especially when I play against AC Milan. That's the club which has really helped me become a star, where I have made many friends. AC Milan will always have a special place in my heart.

Call it a soft spot. I don't know. But don't try and make me a mean person because of what's happened in the past.'

Silvio Berlusconi admitted at the same time, two days before the match, that he had said goodbye to Gullit too early. Berlusconi said: 'I honestly thought Ruud, after his knee operations, had passed his peak and that he was never going to be as good as when he first played for AC Milan. I thought he might have the odd decent game but his incredible performances for Sampdoria have taken me by surprise. He is fantastic, every week I watch him on television. It's been a big mistake to let him go. But that does not change my feelings about him as a person. To me he will be a 'Milanista' forever, even though he wears a different coloured shirt now. And when I see him play, I always want him to win. Except for this Sunday. In our direct confrontation, he has to lose.'

Berlusconi revealed he was disappointed with Gullit for only one reason. The player had promised him he would leave Italy and not sign for another club in *Serie A*. 'Ruud assured me he could never play against AC Milan. He was ready for a move to another country. That's why I allowed him to leave for a small fee. To see him play against AC Milan now, is rather strange. It's a bit unexpected.'

The players of AC Milan had the same feelings. Captain Franco Baresi said, 'Ruud has given so much to this club, that it's strange to be without him. Our opponents used to tremble in the players' tunnel, before we went on to the pitch, if they knew Ruud was standing next to them in an AC Milan shirt. In a way I always felt we were 1–0 up before the match started if Ruud was playing. That's why it will be so difficult to play against him on Sunday. But I have played against my best friends before and I will keep an eye on him. I'll make sure he won't be all that dangerous against us. After all, we are still the league leaders without him.'

But that was not for long. The match in Genoa turned out to be one of the most exciting matches ever seen in Italian football. Some called it the 'match of the decade'. After 72 weeks as league leaders, AC Milan were knocked off the top of *Serie A*, as Sampdoria beat them 3–2, after AC Milan had been leading 2–0 at half-time. In the second half Sampdoria scored twice to get level and in the dying seconds, who else but Ruud Gullit slammed home the winner with a ferocious shot.

Sampdoria were the new leaders in *Serie A* and the stadium in Genoa was rocking on its foundations, with 40,000 fans celebrating and shouting the name of Gullit. It was a miracle, a fairytale which had come true. The next day the Italian newspapers wrote that Frederico Fellini, the famous Italian film director, who died the day before the match, could not have written a better script. The match could have been one of his top productions.

Ruud Gullit was the absolute star of the game. But his old team-mates did not make life easy for him on the pitch. He was tackled, harassed and blatantly kicked. His old pal Costacurta brought him down with a scandalous tackle during the first half. The player was booked, but Gullit still shook hands, got up and carried on as if nothing had happened.

Fabio Capello, who had not been on the best of terms with Gullit in his last season at the club, was angry after the match. He blamed the referee, blew his top about many little things which had gone wrong and showed himself to be a bad loser. The media knew that deep down he could not accept that he had been beaten by the man he did not have a place for in his side.

Gullit did not go out and celebrate that night. He stayed calm and modest. 'It was a lovely goal,' he said, 'It's something you dream of before a match. But I don't need to be in the limelight on my own. I play in a team and all my fellow players at Sampdoria worked incredibly hard.'

The game was one of Gullit's greatest. He is a big match player and when the going gets tough, Gullit gets going. The bigger the pressure, the better he will play. Every time people knock him, count him out or say he is no longer the same player as before, he goes out and shows them he still belongs among the best in the world.

Capello should have known this. In all the important matches during his spell at Milan, as well as under his predecessor Arrigo Sacchi, Gullit was the dominating figure at the club. Every time they were threatened by other teams in *Serie A*, Gullit would put in a dazzling performance. In European Cup Finals, Gullit gave a pep-talk to the players in the dressing room, motivated them on the pitch and took charge during the matches. He played as if there was no pressure at all, while others would tremble.

At Sampdoria he was again a guarantee of success. Gullit hauled Sampdoria back into Europe by winning the Italian Cup.

Success followed Gullit throughout his Italian career but his time there took its toll on him. On more than one occasion he felt exhausted at the end of an Italian season. Tired from the physical and mental demands of *Serie A*. Gullit says: 'Some years I had to cope with operations, getting back to fitness and fighting to get back in the team as quick as possible. Yes, there was always pressure on me in Italy. More than on anybody else in the team. People expect so much from me. Mainly because I am Ruud Gullit. Some players can have a quiet match now and again. Nobody notices or pays attention to it. The media will not write about it. But when your name is Ruud Gullit, you can never have a quiet match. You cannot even have a quiet moment in a match, because people will notice it and they will write about it. In a way that haunts me. I try to do other things when I am not playing football or when I am not training. You have to feel relaxed and free in the mind. But at the end of the day, when the season ends in May or June, I do feel exhausted in my head. More than in the rest of my body.'

To help him cope with the enormous pressure he was often under he would turn to one of the most important people in his life – Dutch sports psychiatrist Ted Troost. At PSV Eindhoven Gullit had worked very closely with Troost. He had originally started as a physiotherapist and manual therapist, but had specialised in the field of sports psychiatry. Troost was looked upon as if he was some kind of strange magician in his own country. Nobody knew exactly whether his therapy was right and medically proven, but for Gullit he became the most influential and charismatic person in his career. And not just for Gullit. Marco van Basten, who also worked very closely with Troost, described the relationship with the psychiatrist like this: 'I am a Formula One car. Ted Troost is the chief mechanic. Without the mechanic the car won't drive and will not win races. Only Ted knows how to tune the car and its engine to perfection.'

The medical staff at the Dutch Football Federation were not very happy with the fact that all the top players consulted Troost in 1987 and 1988. When Dutch FA-doctor Frits Kessel criticised the way Troost tried to cure the best players in the Holland squad, Ruud hit out in an amazing interview with *Nieuwe Revue*. In August 1988 Gullit explained that Troost was the secret key behind the success of the Dutch national team, PSV Eindhoven's European Cup run and the gold medals of some of the Dutch speed skaters at the Olympic games.

Gullit said: 'PSV Eindhoven won the European Cup in May 1988 and more than half of the squad was consulting Ted Troost. Every player had asked for his help individually. Dutch club FC Groningen was about to be relegated to the First Division. They asked for Ted's help and they stayed up in the Premier League. Yvonne van Gennip, Holland's best female speed skater, won three gold medals at the Olympics after she had started to see Ted Troost.

'When the Dutch national football team lost its first match in the Finals of the European Nations Championship, I was already in touch with Troost. Almost every player told me they wanted him with the team. So we approached him and he joined us in Dusseldorf, where Holland had their training camp. Ted Troost became the motivating factor behind the team.

'It is not a coincidence that Holland won all their remaining matches. I dare say that his therapy and his approach had worked all those other times with the top sportsmen in Holland. We became European Champions but I know the Dutch FA were not happy that Ted Troost was involved.'

With Troost's help, Ruud survived the worst periods in his career. Gullit has often spoken about the fact that his career was threatened many times by severe knee injuries; every time Ted guided him and helped him through.

In the summer of 1988, a couple of months after the European Championships, he feared that he would be sidelined again for a long time. At a press conference in Noordwijk aan Zee, a village on the Dutch coast where the national team prepared for international games, Gullit explained the role of Troost.

'I had suffered with a knee injury for many weeks. I was in constant agony. As a player I had to go through the normal procedures at AC Milan. I was getting physiotherapy, daily massage and laser therapy. But nothing seemed to get things right, even though we were convinced I did not need another operation. Like most times, when I was down, I decided to call Ted Troost. He flew from Holland to Milan and gave my knee treatment for three consecutive days. The fourth day I could run, shoot and turn again as if nothing had happened.

'All the doctors and physiotherapists at Milan thought there was something wrong with my cartilage. But Ted Troost knew within a couple of hours of treatment that there was nothing wrong in my knee. It had to do with the muscles in my thigh, they were not strong enough. All my muscles were tensed and stuck together towards my knee. I had been running differently because I had tried to spare my knee.'

According to Gullit the staff of AC Milan watched Troost during those three days, 'with their mouths open'. He explained: 'They were amazed because he has a totally different approach. Before he starts to look at patients or players, he grabs them by their neck, stomach or back. He looks at their spine and the way they run on the pitch. He can diagnose from a distance that certain injuries are caused because of the way they are running or moving.

'We had this player at AC Milan, who had a severe back injury. Ted Troost was asked to see him. He felt his back with his huge, strong hands and said within a couple of minutes that this player had a slipped disc. The doctors were stunned because they needed X-rays to confirm his diagnosis.'

A couple of years later, in a Christmas interview with the left wing magazine, *Vrij Nederlan* (December 1992) Gullit spoke again about his trust and relationship with Troost. He said: 'Ted Troost is more than a friend. We have more than just a bond. We have something very special. When I am with Ted I can do what I want and I can express myself better than with anybody else. I can shout at him, I can swear at him and he can shout and swear at me.

'Ted is the only person who can read my diary. I know it seems odd, to share so much with another person. To have somebody close to you, who you like so much and who is important in your life. Ted is clever. He always has a goal. He knows better than anyone how to get the best out of me. He uses the dialogue to bring a certain energy, frustrations or emotions out into the open.

'Ted has one phrase, which he will throw at me in every situation: "Everything is allowed". What does he mean by that? I can't really explain. All I know is that he is right. There are no rules in this world. People do what they want to do. It might harm me or you, but "everything is allowed".'

CHAPTER TEN

World Stage

In 1980 Holland had a pretty miserable European Championship in Italy. The Dutch team was packed full of stars like Johan Cruyff, Johan Neeskens and Wim van Hanegem, but they were coming to the end of their careers. The Dutch national team no longer had the power they showed in the 1970s which took them to successive World Cup Finals. When Kees Rijvers took over as national coach in the summer of 1981, he thought it was time to bring fresh blood into the team. Ruud Gullit had only just made his name in Dutch football and was still with FC Haarlem. However, Rijvers was so impressed with Gullit's talents that he brought him into the Dutch squad as soon as he was in charge.

On 1 September 1981 Gullit celebrated his 19th birthday. Holland's national coach could not have given him a better present than a place in the Dutch team, which played Switzerland that night in Zurich. At the time the name of Gullit had no significance in other countries, with only the Dutch realising that a wonderboy had entered international football. Europe was not aware of the significance of 1 September 1981, the start of a glorious time for Ruud Gullit in the national team, which would end almost thirteen years later after 63 caps.

Of course, Gullit's international debut would not have been complete if his best friend, Frank Rijkaard, had not joined him.

The two players who started off in the streets of Amsterdam, kicking a ball against brick walls both made their debuts for Holland against the Swiss. However, with so many new young internationals, Holland could not quite make an impact. They lost the match 2–1. For Gullit it was more an experience to play at international level and to see what was expected from him. He did not score, although he came on in an attacking role.

Five weeks later, Gullit played his second international game for Holland in Eindhoven. In the Philips Stadium, 30,000 people turned up to see the impressive youngster outshine other internationals in the game against Greece. Holland won the match 1–0 and afterwards coach Rijvers said how pleased he was with Gullit's performance. 'It won't be long before this lad is going to impress Europe and the world. He needs a few more games but already he is playing for his country as if he has played for them for years. Gullit has no fear, he is stronger than any other player, his pace is electrifying and the power of his shots frightens goalkeepers.'

The first test for Gullit at international level was Holland's bid to qualify for the European Championship to be held in France in 1984. In their first group match, Holland had been disappointing against Iceland, in Reykjavik, where they drew 1–1. If they wanted to go to the European Championships they had to get a good result against Ireland in their second match in Rotterdam. The Irish, who were one of the major contenders with Belgium and Spain in the group, had David O'Leary, Liam Brady, Frank Stapleton and Mark Lawrenson in their side. But none of them were able to stop the impressive Gullit in Rotterdam. The Irish were beaten 2–1 and the second goal for Holland was Ruud Gullit's first for his country.

Slowly but steadily Europe's best players became acquainted with the new Dutch giant, who was making headlines almost

Above: The Italian Job for the three Dutchmen, Gullit, Van Basten and Rijkaard, seen here training with AC Milan.

Below: The AC Milan team of the late eighties, with Gullit and his two fellow Dutchmen as their inspiration, would become one of the greatest club sides in Europe.

Above: Greatness achieved. AC Milan win the European Champions Cup in 1989 and there was no more fitting man to hold the famous trophy aloft than their dreadlocked Dutchman.

Left: High hopes for the Dutch team in Italia '90 as Ruud discusses tactics with national coach Leo Beenhakker at the team's training camp.

Ruud's parents Ria Dil and George Gullit at their son's wedding on 15 May 1994.

Ruud looking dapper in his wedding suit for the big day – his second marriage to Christina Pensa, a student he met and married in Italy.

At last, a son ... second wife Christina with Ruud's baby boy Quincy in 1993.

AC Milan sell Ruud to Sampdoria … discover they can't do without him and take him back … then Ruud ends his Italian success story back with Sampdoria alongside David Platt.

Above: Arriving at Stamford Bridge for the announcement of his transfer from Sampdoria. Hardly anyone at the club could believe it, except Glenn Hoddle. Ruud dons his No 4 shirt for the first time, but Hoddle politely refused to wear a Gullit wig!

Below: The kids' expressions says it all. Ruud really is here, and yes, he is playing for Chelsea. His first pre-season warm-up game on 25 July 1995 attracted so many adoring fans, it was the first time in his life that he didn't have room to warm-up!

Above: What a debut! Ruud is an instant hit in a pre-season friendly as a sweeper. Already he has made his mark in the English game ... and the season hasn't even started yet.

Below: Dennis Bergkamp cost Arsenal £7.5 million while Gullit was a free transfer – but the Chelsea man wins the battle of the world-class Dutchmen playing in the Premier League.

Like Jurgen Klinsmann, Ruud failed to reach the FA Cup Final but got as far as the semi-finals in his inaugural season in English football.

Above: The end of the FA Cup dream, and a hug from Eric Cantona after Manchester United went through at Villa Park in a thrilling semi-final. The Frenchman would go on to pip Gullit for the end-of-season Footballer of the Year award.

Below: Ruud captured the imagination of the English football public with his down to earth and common sense opinions on the game – some of them quite controversial.

every week now. In his next game for Holland, a friendly against France in Rotterdam, the opposition was formed by Michel Platini, Amoros, Tigana and other French stars like Tresor and Fernandez. Holland lost 2–1, but afterwards Platini, who scored the winner eight minutes before the end, spoke highly of one man in the Dutch team. 'Who is the young boy on the wing? He is a lovely player. I like his pace and his tricks. Good shot too. I have rarely seen players of his size who can control the ball like him. He is a real giant, but a beautiful giant to watch. Yes, I'll look out for him when I see Holland play again on television.'

Almost a year and five international games later, on the 12th of October 1983, Holland faced a horrendous task when they journeyed out to Dublin to try and beat the Irish. By this time Gullit was showing his class every week for Feyenoord and starting to become an influential character in the Dutch team. At the age of 21 he was the most dominating figure in the national side.

In Dublin the stadium was packed with 35,000 roaring Irish fans, who were prepared to give the Dutch a warm welcome. Gullit was not impressed, nor frightened. His team-mates, however, froze because of the noise, the atmosphere and the ferocious way the Irish started the match. Within 35 minutes Ireland were 2–0 up with goals from Waddock and Brady.

At half-time the Dutch coach tried to shake up the players. Gullit told them to start playing the Dutch passing game again and also made it clear that they had to give the ball to him a lot more than in the first half. In the second half Gullit's performance was so exciting that even the Irish fans were impressed. On his own Gullit changed the whole match. He scored Holland's first goal, created a second for Marco van Basten and finally Gullit scored the winner.

'Horror story', 'Heartbreak for Republic' and 'Dutch star's

double ends Republic run' were the headlines in the British papers the next day. Every Irish or English reporter gave all the credit to Gullit, 'who was everywhere in Dalymount Park'.

It was in this match that Gullit really showed for the first time at international level how dangerous he could be when he started to make his long runs from the back. In the first half Gullit had played like a sweeper, in the second half he was allowed to go forward. 'Every time he started to run with the ball, our defence looked like sponge,' Ireland manager Eoin Hand said. 'That boy is going to be a world class player. It was a crazy game, but because of Gullit the Dutch team sometimes looked like the famous side from the seventies again. He really is an inspirational figure in the Dutch side.'

A month later Gullit was again the key player for the Dutch. In their one but last European qualifying game they beat Spain 2–1 in Rotterdam, Gullit again scoring the winner. Despite his enormous contribution the Dutch did not manage to qualify for the finals of the European Championship in France. The Spanish had one game left in the group. They had to beat Malta by 11 goals to go through. The inevitable happened. They won 12–1 and the Dutch were literally robbed of their ticket to the finals. The whole nation was shocked and accused the Spanish of bribery. Millions had watched the game live on television.

That night Gullit had not even stayed in the house. 'I went out on a days shopping in Paris with Yvonne. I could not see the point of watching the game on television. Whether it had ended in 1–1 or 12–1, I was not able to change the scoreline from my seat, was I?'

Looking back on 1983 Gullit did admit it had been a marvellous year for him. Qualifying for the European championships would have made it an even more significant occasion. 'But I can't complain about everything that has happened to me this year. The nicest experience of all was the match in Dublin. Yes, because of my individual success out there, but also because of the fabulous atmosphere. For the first time I visited Ireland and was confronted with the madness of football fans in Dublin. Losing 2–0 and finally winning the game 3–2 does not happen to a player at international level a lot.'

In the summer of 1984 Rinus Michels, 'the general', took over from Kees Rijvers. Michels' job was to guide Holland to the World Cup in Mexico. In its group, Holland had to compete with Hungary, Austria, Cyprus and Bulgaria. They finished second in their group and were forced to go into the play-offs with Belgium for one place in Mexico. Holland lost the first game 1–0 and won the second game 2–1 in Rotterdam. On the away goals rule Holland were knocked out. Gullit had had a frustrating year with the national team. At club level everything had gone right for him. His transfer to PSV Eindhoven had turned into a very successful move. With PSV he was competing for the League Championship and individually he was performing extremely well. But at international level the group matches for the World Cup in Mexico became the only qualifying period in his entire career where Gullit never scored.

To make matters worse, Rinus Michels had to retire as national coach for three months because of heart trouble. Again the Dutch FA did not approach Johan Cruyff but instead Leo Beenhakker, who had never played professional football in his life. Beenhakker was only in charge of the national team for three international games, against Cyprus, Austria and Hungary. Gullit played in only one of these matches.

When Rinus Michels took over again Gullit was more than pleased. He developed a very good understanding with Michels, who had strong character and who was considered as one of the best coaches in Dutch football. After all he was the man who took Holland to the World Cup final in 1974 with 'total football'.

Gullit felt he and Michels could get the Orange-machine working again with new, superb talents like Marco van Basten, Frank Rijkaard, Ronald Koeman and himself. It did work. The Dutch qualified gloriously for the Euro '88 finals in Germany.

Despite losing in the first match against Russia, Holland dominated that tournament. Gullit had just won the Italian League championship with AC Milan in his first season in *Serie A*, but he was strong enough to play a vital part in Holland's national team in Germany. In Dusseldorf he and Marco van Basten tormented England. Van Basten scored a hat-trick, but Gullit created all the danger on the wing and in attack. In the final, Ruud Gullit scored the first goal against Russia, Marco van Basten got the second one. After the final whistle Gullit ran to Rinus Michels and for the first time in his career he lifted his coach on his own shoulders and danced around the pitch with him.

Unfortunately for Gullit, Rinus Michels decided to step down. The new national coach was Thijs Libregts, a well known figure to Gullit and anything but a popular choice. Libregts had worked with Gullit at Feyenoord. Despite winning the Dutch League Championship with Libregts, Gullit had had a very cool relationship with this manager.

The main reason for this was an incident in the media. In his time as Feyenoord manager, Libregts had made some very uncomplimentary remarks about Gullit in an interview in a national newspaper. Libregts criticised Gullit's workrate. In the eyes of the manager he was brilliant one moment and strolling around on the pitch the next, 'But you know what it's like with those blacks,' Libregts said, 'They have that sort of attitude.' Although Libregts played the incident down many times and even tried to discuss the subject with his star player, Gullit never forgot the remarks. Libregts was to pay the penalty six years later. After a brilliant qualifying run for the World Cup finals in Italy, Libregts thought there would be few, if any, problems. Holland had qualified for the first time unbeaten for the World Cup. But all through the campaign, Gullit had criticised the style of play. In 1989 he had spent most of his time in hospital or at the physio. Sometimes he had to pull out of the international games at the last minute. But his criticism of the team's tactics was always there, and often very well founded.

To Gullit it was clear that there was not much wrong with the team and the players, but they needed a different coach if they wanted to become World Champions. The name of Johan Cruyff was on every player's lips, including Marco van Basten's and Gullit's. As Libregts was not prepared to step down, Gullit called for a meeting of the players before a game in Finland. Libregts was asked by Gullit if he could leave the changing room in the stadium in Helsinki. The manager must have known what Gullit's ideas were. The players, captained by Gullit, decided to keep quiet about their frustrations and unhappiness with Libregts in charge.

The players agreed to vote at a later stage about asking the FA to sack Thijs Libregts. At the Hilton Hotel at Schiphol's airport in Amsterdam a month later the verdict came. The majority of the players were not prepared to go to the World Cup with Libregts as national manager. The Dutch media were full of headlines for weeks about the 'players' power.'

For the Dutch FA it was a difficult matter to solve. They had hardly any grounds on which they could sack Libregts. The coach immediately told the FA directors he refused to go and even took the FA to court. He insisted he would keep his job. Libregts was outraged, 'I had done the best qualifying job in many years. I guided Holland to the World Cup finals, which was the only job the FA asked me to do when I was approached two years before.

We even finished above Germany in our group, which meant it was not an easy group either. What makes the FA think they have to listen to a few players and sack me?' But the FA won their battle in court, claiming there was a 'bad atmosphere between the coach and the players'. The court in Utrecht decided the FA had a point and it was impossible for Libregts to keep his job.

However, when Rinus Michels, technical advisor of the Dutch FA, was asked to find a replacement for the World Cup he did not turn to Johan Cruyff. Leo Beenhakker was his surprise choice. The reason was obvious with Johan Cruyff and Rinus Michels anything but the best of friends. Michels did not want Cruyff to run the FA. It would be easier with Beenhakker in charge; however, the players were angry. They admitted they had not formerly asked Michels to approach Cruyff first, but they had mentioned to him and the other members of the FA that Cruyff was on top of their list.

The whole thing left a lot of scars in the Dutch squad and caused a bad atmosphere in the camp when the Holland party boarded the plane which took them to Italy. Ruud Gullit was annoyed with Rinus Michels and half way through the tournament their conflicts erupted on a training pitch in Palermo, on the island of Sicily.

The FA had ordered everyone in the Dutch squad not to speak to the media during training sessions in Sicily. On the morning after the game between Holland and Egypt, Michels decided to take Dutch sports writer Dick van den Polder with him and sat down in the dug out for a major newspaper interview. At the time the players were training under Leo Beenhakker on the same pitch.

When Gullit saw Michels in the dug out with the journalist he shouted for the press officer and sent him with a clear message to Michels. Dick van den Polder, the journalist says he will never forget the incident. 'Michels was ordered off the park by Gullit. He claimed that the rules applied to everyone in the Dutch camp, including Rinus Michels. The press officer did not know what to do. Michels took no notice and wanted to carry on with the interview which we did. But Gullit's face looked like a thunderstorm. The whole atmosphere out there was very bad.'

Holland were knocked out of the finals in the second round by Germany after a major incident between Gullit's team-mate Frank Rijkaard and Rudi Voller. After the World Cup Rinus Michels took charge of the national team himself again, still keeping Johan Cruyff out in the cold. Michels took Dick Advocaat on as his assistant and made it clear that Advocaat was going to be trained to take over as national manager after the European Championship in Sweden in 1992.

Although Gullit was captain of the national side, he could not play a major part in the next qualifying stages for the European Championships. In May 1991 he had another severe knee injury. Marc Martens, the Belgian specialist who had operated three times before on the same right knee, took a piece of cartilage out. Gullit missed the end of the season and had to work hard to make a comeback in time for the 1991/92 season.

In Sweden, the following summer, Holland had a good tournament, but they failed to reach the final. In the semi-final Holland were knocked out by Denmark, with Marco van Basten missing from the spot in the penalty shoot-out.

After the European Championships in Sweden, Rinus Michels resigned as national manager and handed the job over to Dick Advocaat. Holland were drawn in the same group as England for the qualifying rounds for the 1994 World Cup. Gullit looked forward to the clashes with England for two reasons. He had very good memories of other games against them. He had never lost against England at international level (Euro '88, Italia '90) and he was eager to play at Wembley. In almost 15 years of professional football Gullit had only played at Wembley once. In March 1988 he played for Holland in a match against England which ended 2–2, but Gullit had to come off in the second half with an injury.

As much as Gullit had looked forward to playing at Wembley, the 1992 game against England turned into one of the biggest humiliations of his career. England took the lead with a stunning free-kick from John Barnes then David Platt scored a second. Dennis Bergkamp brought Holland back into the game, but Advocaat was not happy with the performance of the team. He could have taken off any player, but he decided to substitute Gullit after an hour. Gullit was totally shocked that Advocaat thought he was not important enough for the team any longer. When Gullit walked the long way to the dressing rooms at Wembley, the only fans who applauded him were the English supporters. The Dutch never gave him a chant. That night looked to be the end of Gullit's international career. Within a week he announced that he would no longer play for his country. He wanted to stick to league matches for Sampdoria.

Advocaat accepted it. For the remaining qualifying matches Advocaat never called upon Gullit any more. But not long before the finals of the World Cup in the United States he felt as if he could not do without him. The Dutch media had put pressure on the coach too. They reported every weekend about Gullit's terrific performances with Sampdoria.

Advocaat travelled to Italy, had a long chat with Gullit and decided to bring him back into the national team. Gullit joined the Dutch squad in Noordwijk, where they had their training camp before the World Cup. When he arrived there, nobody knew that Gullit had only agreed to return under certain conditions and he did not agree with the playing style of the Dutch team.

The Dutch had only one friendly game left in Holland before they flew to America. They played Scotland in Utrecht and Gullit played brilliantly as ever on the wing. At half-time he came off because Advocaat wanted to use more players.

After the match Gullit appeared on television. When a Dutch TV reporter asked him what he thought of the game, Gullit was very critical. He thought the whole match was disappointing and did not live up to his expectations. Eyebrows were raised, nobody knew what Gullit meant. The match had been quite exciting. His own performance was very satisfying and the Scots hardly had a touch of the ball in the first half.

Five days later, only three weeks before the start of the World Cup in America, more than a hundred press people from more than ten different countries turned up for a major press conference in Hotel Huis ter Duin on the Dutch coast.

When Dick Advocaat sat down behind the table and grabbed a microphone, Ger Stolk, the press officer, came in. Behind him was Ruud Gullit, in jeans and with his head bowed. Gullit joined Advocaat behind the microphones. The room went quite and all the reporters were stunned when Advocaat coolly announced, 'Ruud Gullit is not playing for Holland in the World Cup. He is leaving our hotel and going home this morning.'

Gullit looked very emotional. His eyes looked sad, although his voice was calm. At first nobody knew what to say. Nor did Gullit. He continued to look down. He mumbled and hesitated before his first words emerged. 'I don't feel very good about all this. But take it from me it has been a very emotional decision. Usually I can handle myself very well with the press. But not this time. I can hardly express my feelings.'

Every single journalist held his breath. It was still a major shock. Clive Tyldesly, who was in the room for a BBC World Cup special, wanted to stop the camera filming. 'This is not much good. What's going on? It's a very strange press conference.'

A Dutch journalist quickly told Clive, who had not understood a word of all the Dutch phrases, to keep his cameras going, 'Don't stop filming! I'll translate things later. This is a very emotional moment in the career of Ruud Gullit!'

Gullit looked, for the first time, in the face of all the media people. Almost three full minutes had passed and still nobody had dared put a question to him. Everyone just waited for Gullit to come out with more words, more of an explanation. Gullit realised they were desperate for him to tell more. He did, although it did not make things clearer. 'Please, believe me. I really did want to go to the World Cup. I really wanted to show something in America. I wanted to go out there and play fabulous football. But I honestly cannot tell you all at this moment why I have taken this decision.

'I understand you want to know, and the public want to know what has made me do this. But I can't and I don't want to go into details. The team is in the middle of a very important preparation time for the World Cup finals. For the team and the rest of the squad it is better that I don't spill too many beans. I don't want to cause a lot of trouble. I don't want you lot to blow the whole thing up either.'

A Dutch TV reporter uttered the first question from the back of the room: 'Could you please tell us if your decision has anything to do with the team?'

Gullit, softly spoken: 'I don't want to go into details.'

'But surely that is not a detail. Is it a footballing matter or is your decision a very personal problem?'

Gullit, nodding: 'Yes, for me it's a personal matter. I can understand you want an answer. But take it from me, it's not an easy thing to walk out of the Dutch camp like this. But I could not possibly stay any longer. I wish the lads a lot of success out there.

And I realise it will be a whole different World Cup for Holland now.'

The reporter was still not satisfied: 'What on earth has created this strange situation?'

Gullit: 'I came back in the squad after a long absence. I wanted to see how things were again. What sort of atmosphere I would meet and how the team would play. I tried to keep calm and watch from a distance. I wanted to weigh up the situation without taking charge straight away.'

'Not take charge? You always take charge. Not because you want to, but you are a born leader. Besides that we could not notice a different attitude. You seemed to be training happily, you were talking to the players.'

Gullit: 'Mmmhhh ... I did talk to some players, yes.'

'We still thought you were very enthusiastic when you arrived here in Holland.'

Gullit: 'Enthusiastic? Me? You should have listened better to things I said after the game against Scotland. I analysed our game in a proper way. Look, I have been in Italy long enough and I have played at the top level long enough to know what is good and bad in international football. I saw totally different things than the public or the press in our game against Scotland. I was not happy about that. But the next morning after I had spoken out on TV, the papers were going mad. I will tell Dick Advocaat after the World Cup what the real reason was why I quit.'

The newspaper reporters had now sensed that Gullit was prepared to talk about certain things and started to dive in with questions.

Gullit, shaking his broad shoulders once more, 'You can write or say what you want. It does not bother me. Because I don't give a reason for my sudden departure, I'll have to accept that people will start writing or saying silly things. But all I want to add to it is this: I don't quit because I can't play football or because I feel as if I am not able to play a major part in the team during the finals.'

One Dutch journalist was getting frustrated with the way the press conference was going. Gullit, however, did not care and sat very quiet, still next to the manager, Dick Advocaat. The journalist had a go at Gullit: 'Don't you think you are getting vaguer every minute?'

Gullit, for the first time slightly irritable: 'Just say and write what you want.'

'Have you told the manager why you are leaving?'

Gullit: 'No. He'll be the first person I'll tell when he comes back from the World Cup.'

'You quit before, but you made a comeback. Is this your final resignation?'

Gullit: 'I'm leaving now and I will never, never play for Holland again.'

The first TV reporter was coming back into the conversation. He wanted to know if the players and the manager should have acted quicker when he came out with strong criticism of the Dutch team after the game against Scotland. 'If we look back now, you were a frustrated man during that game and even more afterwards. Is that why you have decided to leave?'

Gullit: 'Not really. I have often given my views on a game in the past. I did the same thing this time. Although I must admit that, once I had analysed the game properly, I made some conclusions.'

'Did the players not think you went over the top with your criticism of the way the team played against Scotland?'

Gullit: 'Nobody has come up to me to tell me that.'

'Four years ago you made a mistake. You were unhappy with the situation around the Dutch team. Beenhakker was appointed as national manager for the World Cup in Italy. The players, including you, wanted Johan Cruyff. You decided to stick to the team, but deep down in your heart you preferred to leave Italy. You did not and you did not play a very good tournament. Were you frightened you were going to make the same mistake?'

Gullit: 'I don't want to comment on that. All I did after the game against Scotland was express my feelings. I did not go into details about the team tactics.'

'Just try and tell us with one answer why you are so frustrated with everything at this moment.'

Gullit: 'Look, don't force me. The whole thing is depressing me enough as it is. I don't want to explain anything at this moment. I am leaving. I am going back to Milan. That's where my future is. Not with the Dutch national team.'

Gullit got up and walked out the hotel into a Dutch friend's car. Cameramen tried to follow him, but they lost him before Gullit was out of the village of Noordwijk.

In the hotel the other players could not believe what had gone on. When they had been informed at breakfast by Dick Advocaat, the feelings in the Dutch camp were very mixed. Ulrich van Gobbel, a big Surinam born defender, who was a close pal of Gullit, said he was totally devastated. 'I can't tell you what a blow this is for the team. I hate it. I wish this had never happened. Ruud is such a wonderful man to have in the team. He is a brilliant player, but he is a motivator, a binding factor too. He can carry the whole team on his shoulders. It has only just happened and I know everyone feels the same. But I tell you now that everyone will admit in the United States how much we will miss him.'

Ronald Koeman tried to stop Gullit from going. The Barcelona defender had gone to Gullit's hotel room when Advocaat told him first what was happening. Koeman said: 'I ran straight to his room. He let me in and we talked. I was hoping I could make him stay. But I could see on his face that he had already decided to go. I even begged him to tell me why he was doing this. 'Is it the team, is it the coach? Just tell us what it is so we can stop you from going, Ruud.' But he did not want to answer those questions. 'Whatever is bugging you, tell me Ruud. I am prepared to do anything to solve your problems.' But again I got no answer from him.'

Even Gullit's best friend Frank Rijkaard, was shocked by the news. 'I do think I know him quite well. In the first week of our training camp, I did not sense any troubles. He usually pulls a moody face if something is bothering him. But he did not do that this time. I thought he was alright. But apparently something must have frustrated him. As I was not able to speak to him before he went, I don't want to judge him. All I know is that it is a great loss for the Dutch team in the World Cup.'

Ronald Koeman was much stronger in his judgements. Koeman did think Gullit had let the team down. 'I am very disappointed in Ruud,' said Koeman. 'Especially because the coach tried everything to keep him happy. Gullit was allowed to play where he wanted in the team. He did not have to join the talking sessions of the older players with the coach before important games. He was not given any strict rules in the hotel either. Really, he could do what he liked.'

Whereas Gullit, who rejoined his wife Christina Pensa and his children in Italy, refused to explain why he had made such a strong decision, 10,000 miles away from Holland somebody else did lift the curtain of secrecy. George Gullit, Ruud's father who was living in Paramaribo, the capital of Surinam, gave Dutch journalists a strong hint about his son's decisions to retire from international football.

'I knew right from the beginning,' George said on the terrace of his villa in Paramaribo, 'That it could not lead to anything positive. I did not agree with Ruud's return to the Dutch squad in the first place. I told him that and he knows this. The way Holland play, the sickening arrogance of the Ajax players and the bad atmosphere in the team, it was all too negative for Ruud to be happy in the Dutch squad.

'I haven't spoken to him yet,' George Gullit continued on the morning of 31 May, less than 24 hours after his son's decision to go quit the Dutch camp. 'But I do think I know what it is all about. And not very often I am wrong!

'Last week I spoke to him on the telephone for ages. We had a good chat about him playing again for the national team. I said, 'Ruud, pack it in? Why are you going back to a situation you don't like? Too much has happened in the past. The Ajax-players are dominating the squad. They have only just arrived at international level and they think they know it all.' Ruud wouldn't listen. But now, a week later, everything has gone the way I predicted.

'My son has won almost every trophy a professional player can win in this world. So how on earth can Ajax captain Danny Blind dare come out with a statement, saying: 'Ruud can come back in the team if he is fit and in form again.' Who the hell is Danny Blind? All I read in newspapers and magazines are his words: 'We are Ajax, we are the best.'

'My boy won't even think about playing for a team where the stupid ones and inexperienced ones are in charge. It's the terror of the Ajax-part of the national team which is ruining the atmosphere. It's a bomb under the success of the Dutch side. And Dick Advocaat, the manager, is accepting it all.'

George Gullit was convinced the Ajax players hated to see Gullit come back to the national team. They had qualified for the World Cup without him and they were sure they could also be successful in the USA without Gullit. George also criticised the lack of discipline in the Dutch squad. He said: 'Marco van Basten and Ruud have been brought up with discipline and proper rules. They know how to respect people and to show a good attitude.

According to what I have heard and what I know, the Ajax players have shown no respect at all. Everyone is just messing about in the camp. Ruud does not agree with all that. He can't stand it and he knew all this would never have happened if Johan Cruyff had been in charge.'

George Gullit's words went down well in the media in Holland, who finally got a reasonable explanation for Ruud's walk out. Ruud's father even had a very strong opinion about the tactics of the national team, which he was sure had frustrated his son too. 'It bothers Ruud that no one wants to listen to him. The coach should have discussed things with him. Ruud has played more finals at international level than anyone else in the Dutch squad. And definitely more than his manager, who never played for his country. Yes, Ruud does support attacking football. But you can't attack like Holland do in the extreme heat in Florida, Dallas, Washington and Los Angeles, where matches will kick off at 12 o'clock in the afternoon. I spoke about this with Ruud and we both said it would be suicidal to play with four men up front like Holland always do.

'All my son was trying to make clear was that Holland should be more realistic if they wanted to win the World Cup. They had to change their tactics to compete with the best teams in the world. But you know why Dick Advocaat did not want to do that? Because the Ajax players were telling him they did not agree with Ruud's views. They wanted to stick to the Ajax system, which Advocaat had adopted for the national team.

'I am glad Ruud has quit. It was the best thing he could do. My son is not naive. He is not going to have a go at the World Cup if he knows beforehand that he could never win it.'

CHAPTER ELEVEN

Private Life: The Man Behind the Dreadlocks

L ittle is known about Ruud Gullit's private life. Although he has always had a very good understanding with the majority of the media, he has tried to keep his private affairs out of the limelight. He has carefully protected his homes, his wives and his children from newspaper photographers and newsmen. Only occasionally would he allow a Dutch photographer like Peter Smoulders to take pictures of his family in the house or in the garden.

However, for the media there was still plenty to write about, as Ruud has not exactly lead a quiet life off the pitch. He has been married twice, had an affair with an Italian female sportswriter who worked on one of Silvio Berlusconi's newspapers, became a successful singer with the band Revelation Time and has campaigned against racism and apartheid.

Ruud's first wife, Yvonne de Vries, is the same age as him. She had been his girlfriend since the age of 16. He had got to know her at school and she moved with him to Rotterdam, when he signed his first big contract with Feyenoord. The couple were married on 30th August 1984. The wedding took place in the countryside village of Alpen aan de Rijn, about 30 miles from Amsterdam. His best man was Wim van Hanegem. Even though the wedding took place on a Friday and Feyenoord had a league match on the

Sunday, the whole squad turned up for what turned out to be one of the biggest wedding parties in the football world. Ruud made it a fabulous reggae-party and he got all the celebrities who were present dancing to Bob Marley. Revelation Time also performed on the night. And of course the party would not have been complete if the player himself had not climbed on stage. In his wedding suit he was handed the microphone and sang his own Top 20 hit song, 'Not The Dancing Kind'.

Asked where he was going on honeymoon, Gullit said (at four o'clock in the morning): 'I think we have got a four-hour coach trip to Kerkrade, for our first away game of the season .'

The following year, on 12 December 1985, Ruud and Yvonne had their first child, a daughter, called Felicity. Two years later they had another girl, called Sharmayne.

Ruud asked Yvonne what she thought about moving to Italy when, in December 1986, the initial interest from AC Milan was made public. Yvonne said she would do anything for Ruud and would follow him anywhere in the world. It made it easy for him to conduct talks with Silvio Berlusconi in the spring of 1987.

As he became a megastar, the interest from the media and the Italian newspapers in particular, intensified. After his first twelve months in Italy every little detail about his football career had been revealed. Next on the agenda was his private life. Among the multitude of reporters who followed Ruud Gullit's exploits was one female journalist, Lici Granelli. Ruud had a good understanding with her. But in the newspapers she was described as 'the black mistress of the AC Milan star'.

Ruud was bitterly upset, and as a result of that kind of publicity, he refused to talk to the media for three months. But in an exclusive television interview on one of Silvio Berlusconi's own stations, Gullit spoke in December 1988 about his anger and frustrations.

'It is against my own principles,' Gullit said in front of the TV camera, 'To talk about my private life. That is the only reason why I have not spoken to the media for more than three months. Really, I don't think I should be defending myself against something which is not true. But as people and reporters kept writing and talking about certain aspects of my private life, I am prepared to talk about things.

'A lot of people had warned me about going to Italy and that I would not be able to live a normal life any longer. I would become a victim of the media, the fans and other people around me. I did not believe that. And of course I know that is the price you have to pay when you play for a big club and when they describe you as a star player.

'I still enjoy my life in Italy. I have many new friends. And among all those new friends there is a female friend too. In Holland it is very common that one has male and female friends. Here, in Italy, it's obviously something people are not used to. I cannot believe all the fuss and stories in the papers. I think some male reporters must have been jealous. I bet they were angry that I was spending more time with her after a match than with them.

'It is a result of me not playing for four weeks as well. Because of an injury, I was out of the side. So there was nothing to write about me in the papers. They had to come up with something different ... But, yes, it does annoy me. It does frustrate me that I am being monitored all the time.'

But in August 1989 the rumours about his marriage came to a dramatic climax. Ruud admitted that he was getting divorced from Yvonne. The news was on the front pages of all the Italian sports papers, as well as the normal papers and the Dutch newspapers. It even appeared on the six o'clock television news in both countries.

Gazzetta dello Sport, the biggest sports paper of all, quoted

Gullit's wife, Yvonne saying, 'He was my best friend when we were at school together, then he became my husband, now he is my best friend again. I will stay in Italy and I will carry on living in Milan, because I know Ruud would miss our two little daughters like mad if I moved back to Holland. And I know how hard he finds it to be separated from them. I don't want to do anything that would damage his career. And I know how much it means for him to feel good away from the football pitch. For Ruud it's the most important condition to him performing well on the pitch. He must feel fit, both physically and mentally.'

As well as his divorce, there has further heart-break for Gullit in 1989 when on 7th July there occurred one of the most tragic episodes in his life. In South America, at Zanderij Airport in Surinam, a DC 8 from Surinam Airways crashed. On board were 185 passengers and only 15 survived.

Among the 171 killed was a whole football team from the Dutch Premier League. It was a team which had been formed by black players with Surinam roots. For most of them it was their first visit to the country where they were born. Ruud Gullit had been asked to take part in the tour, against Surinam teams, but was not released by AC Milan and instead spent the summer in Italy. Ruud was devastated when he was told about the loss of his friends. He had played with or against most of the players. He had known every one of them. One of the players was a very close friend, Jerry Haatrecht.

In a memorial service in Amsterdam, soon after the crash, Ruud delivered an emotional speech in front of thousands of people, with millions watching live on TV. 'Jerry,' Gullit said, 'If you hear me, I want you to know we love you,' was the last sentence of his speech. His words were so moving, that they had the audience in tears.

For more than one reason the aeroplane disaster was a tragic moment in Gullit's career. The team, on its way to tour Surinam, was a group of famous, successful footballers. That team had a great impact in the Netherlands, where the government was trying to solve the problem of a society with a big Surinam population attempting to integrate with the white, Dutch people.

In Ruud Gullit, black people in the Netherlands, and through-out Europe, had a successful sportsman to look up to. A star who was prepared to fight against Apartheid and to campaign for all the black people in the world. But Ruud did not want to campaign alone, he needed the players who were part of the team that went to Surinam just as much.

The Dutch team, which reached the finals of the World Cup in 1974 and 1978, did not have a single black player in the squad. After Gullit had achieved international status many other black players were selected by the Dutch FA. Aaron Winter, Bryan Roy, Frank Rijkaard, Clarence Seedorf, Edgar Davids and Patrick Kluivert are only a few of the players who followed in Gullit's footsteps.

Gullit's first confrontation with the hostilities against black people came when he was a 13-year-old schoolboy. With one of his friends, he had been hanging around in a big store. Like many naughty boys of that age, his friend had wanted to pinch a bar of chocolate. After approaching the shelf three or four times, his friend did not have the courage and Ruud decided to leave the shop. As they went through the door, a security man stopped them and took Ruud to the police. He was accused of shoplifting. The other boy was not even asked what he had been up to. Only Ruud Gullit was arrested – because he was black.

When Ruud won the European Footballer of the Year award in 1987, he dedicated his trophy to Nelson Mandela. As the South African ANC leader was in jail at the time, Gullit did not have the chance to meet him. But seven years later, in February 1994, the Dutchman did meet his hero. In a television studio Gullit presented his golden award to Mandela, who he embraced very tightly. He told him how much he appreciated all the hard work Mandela had put in for his campaign against Apartheid.

'It was a dream that became reality,' Gullit said. 'I was very emotional when I was actually with him. But that was not strange. I had been looking forward to meeting him for so many years. Mandela means so much to me and to other young people in the world. He was arrested in 1962 which was the year I was born. It is hard to imagine that someone was in prison almost all the time I was alive.'

Ruud's divorce from Yvonne in 1989 was only the start of the less than welcome stories about his private life in the media and the glossy gossip magazines in Italy. In the summer of 1990, just after the World Cup finals in Italy, the press reported about the fight of Yvonne de Vries for a £1.5 million divorce settlement. She wanted her share from Ruud Gullit's huge income as a player. The £1.5 million, according to the media, was a payment in addition to the annual maintenance money to his children. It was a well known fact that he was already the best paid footballer in the world. He did not only have a big income from AC Milan, but also millions of pounds from sponsorship, appearances and other business projects.

All the bad things come at once, Gullit thought, when in November 1989 he discovered that his luxurious apartment in Milan had been burgled. The thieves stole some of his personal trophies, jewellery, money and art.

Around that time the first stories appeared about the woman who was the new love in his life. Christina Pensa, a blond Italian-born girl, was reported to have taken the place of Yvonne after a string of other, brief relationships. Although he did not get married at once to Christina, she became pregnant and, in March 1991, gave Ruud a son, called Quincy.

On 15 May 1994, Ruud married Christina. For a long time he had tried to keep the wedding date and place a secret. Gullit even fooled journalists by deliberately leaking a date and a place. On the Tuesday before the actual wedding, dozens of photographers assembled outside Milan's town hall. They waited all day, but nothing happened. Despite the fact that he had not appeared in every game for AC Milan in his last season, Ruud was still a megastar to the public and the media. Even a glimpse of him and his bride, a picture taken with a telephoto lens, would make headlines the following day.

It was the arrival of two other football players at the town hall square a couple of days later, which alerted the photographers that their patience would be rewarded. They were two of the biggest names in football. The first to arrive was Jurgen Klinsmann who turned up in a modern, Italian designer suit. Klinsmann and Gullit had always had a good understanding. Despite the fact that Holland and Germany were big rivals on the pitch, they had built up a sound friendship. Their characters, after all, were very much the same. Both had the same political views. They had both campaigned against racism, were supporters of Greenpeace and were both interested in the environment, nuclear issues and similar subjects.

Next was Marco van Basten and his wife. The Dutchman was Gullit's best friend since Frank Rijkaard had left AC Milan. He had not been playing for almost a year himself, but socially was still very close to Gullit. Van Basten often talked with Gullit about the hard battle to regain full fitness. Gullit had been down that road once or twice himself but had been more lucky. Van Basten, though, would never play again.

Another close friend of Gullit's at his wedding was Ted Troost, the Dutch sports psychiatrist from Rotterdam. Besides Klinsmann, Van Basten and Troost, there was only Gullit's family and Christina Pensa's family at the wedding. His dad, George Gullit, had flown over from Surinam, while his mum came from Amsterdam.

Two years after his marriage Ruud had another child with Christina, a daughter called Cheyenne. Even more than before Gullit kept his family life out of the limelight. He had had enough of all the gossip magazines in Italy and the Netherlands. However, he could not stop magazines publishing stories about his stormy marriage with Christina. In July 1995 the first articles appeared saying that he was going to end his second marriage. He was leaving his Italian wife in Genoa to start a new life in London.

Ruud has always been devoted to his children. One of the reasons he moved to London was that it would be a lot closer to his two daughters from his first marriage. From Heathrow he can be in Amsterdam within 50 minutes. Even when he is playing in another country, Ruud is still very concerned about the way his kids grow up. He is constantly aware of their welfare or their problems.

In an interview in *Rotterdam's Dagblad*, he once explained what his ideas are about bringing up young children. Ruud said, 'I grew up in the Jordaan, one of the oldest parts of Amsterdam. My parents told me to look after myself and they gave me a lot of responsibility. In those days that was possible. Everything depends on the circumstances and the surroundings, where a child grows up. I don't think I can do the same things with my children as my parents did with me. Times have changed. The traffic in Amsterdam, Milan or London is a hundred times busier now. The streets are not safe. In Amsterdam, kids will see drugs on the streets, in Milan and London they see tramps. Everything they see or grow up with can have a strong influence on their lives.

'It also depends on the character of the child. Maybe my parents knew I could look after myself. My son Quincy will grow up differently. But I will never bore him with stories about the good old days. If he wants to know one day what life was like in Amsterdam, when I was young, I will tell him. If he does not want to know, that is fine with me.

'I do think it is important which school he goes to. I prefer my boy to be at school where there are lots of cultures, as he can find out for himself at school what the world is like. I am doubtful whether he should go to an Italian or an English school in Italy. None of the kids in Italy speak any English, which I think is a gap in their education. On the other hand I realise he will be at a posh school, if I send him where English is an important subject. And I don't want my kid to feel he belongs to the upper class.

'I also speak Dutch to my boy. The first words I taught him were Dutch words because it is nice for my parents, who don't speak Italian or English. They must be able to converse with him in Dutch. Besides that, I want him to communicate with the two girls in Holland, who live with my ex-wife Yvonne. And of course it is always handy if he can speak more than one language.'

Ruud looks back on his childhood with many happy memories. 'I think I had a wonderful childhood. When I was young I was never aware of the fact that I was black. I only started to realise that when I was about 14 years of age. Until that moment I never had the feeling that I was different.'

He feels he has benefited from the fact that he grew up in a city like Amsterdam. He is a true cosmopolitan. 'I think 'being black' has helped a lot, in fact. Because as a black person I always had to work harder or do more than white kids. Everyone was watching me, they were always wondering how 'the black boy' would do. For me it was a motivating factor.'

In the interview Ruud also explained the real pain of a divorce. Especially because he has so many happy memories of his own childhood, he thinks it must hurt his own children to grow up without their dad. Gullit said: 'For the kids it is really awful. I ring them as often as I can. My two oldest daughters now live in Holland, although I try to have them with me as often as possible. A divorce is a very big step, emotionally and rationally. It is not something you did from one day to another. A lot of things usually happen before it comes to an end of a relationship. But I have always said that it is better to take the wrong decision than no decision at all.

'I don't want to say I took the wrong decision with my first marriage. But I have learnt to accept the consequence of certain decisions in life. For my children it is important to have a stable and happy situation at home. And I think they do feel safe and happy right now.'

The move to Chelsea in the summer of 1995 presented no problems to the globetrotting Gullit. He says, 'I can hardly get over the fact that I love this place so much. I loved the atmosphere and the people instantly. The morning I arrived, I told myself: 'Ruud, you are going to enjoy living here.'

'Besides a couple of football matches and visiting White Hart Lane or Wembley with Feyenoord and the Dutch national team, I hadn't seen much of London. Not even for a holiday, not for a short break or anything else. But after couple of weeks of living here I knew it was a great city.

'With a club like Chelsea I am lucky of course. The stadium is probably in one of the most glamorous and busiest parts of London. The area is fantastic. The way of life in Chelsea is wonderful. The music, the restaurants, the people, I love it all so much. I honestly think it is one of the most fabulous parts of London.

'One of the best things about living in England was that I could express myself from the very first day, nice and clear. I speak the language and it helps you settle in quickly.

'I still don't have the freedom to walk around, dine and drink or shop without fans coming up to me. Wherever I go, people recognise me. But that has happened all through my career. Sometimes that can be frightening, but here I enjoy it. The English people have manners, they are kind and they are warm. And those are the qualities in people I like the best.'

The season ended for Ruud with controversy again surrounding his private life. Something he detests. Ruud was romantically linked with the teenage niece of Johan Cruyff, 18-year-old Estelle Cruyff, a stunning 6 ft blonde. Estelle has known Ruud since she was eight years old but the relationship blossomed when Gullit invited her to celebrate New Year's Eve with his friends at a Dutch nightclub called Sinners In Heaven.

Estelle's father Hennie said in Amsterdam: 'They danced at the disco and – bang – that was it. It happens. Ruud has told me that he likes Estelle very much. As her father, all that matters to me is to see her happy. She is very beautiful and hundreds of men want to go out with her. The point is that I know him, we know his family and I know he is decent.' Hennie, owner of a string of sports shops in Holland, is the elder brother of the seventies World Cup superstar Johan. Hennie said: 'Ruud has been coming in and out of the shop since he was 12. He's a good guy and he's doing well. So why not? Age is not a big issue. They have known each other for years.'

One great 'love' of his life is golf, the best way he feels he can relax away from the pressures of football. He has played some of the finest courses in the country, such as Birkdale and The Belfry, with a handicap of 16 and alongside Alan Hansen, Des Lynam and the rest of the BBC crew. 'I'm the only black man who can beat them!' Ruud bursts into prolonged fits of laughter.

You always feel a warm glow in Ruud's company.

CHAPTER TWELVE

Boss of the Bridge

Chelsea Football Club might have shocked the soccer world when they signed Ruud Gullit before the 1995/96 season, but there was to be an even more remarkable end to Gullit's first year in England when he took on the role of player-manager at Stamford Bridge, the first managerial position of his career.

The departure of Glenn Hoddle, to become England coach, lead to a popular movement for Gullit to be appointed in his place. That mood was clear at the final game of the season against Blackburn at the Bridge – when the Chelsea fans demanded that their hero should be the successor to Hoddle.

The final days of the season had been traumatic for Chelsea after Hoddle had been offered the England job. Ruud was torn between wanting Hoddle to stay, and for his manager to further his career by taking the prestigious FA post. At the time he was being ultra cautious about his comments in this country, however, he was far more forthright in a Dutch TV interview in his native tongue. He said: 'This is the perfect time for Glenn to go into international coaching. He has played all over Europe and he has played at the highest level for England. I do not know a better candidate for the job in English football. He couldn't wish for a better moment and a bigger chance. When I say this I am thinking of what is best for Glenn.

'I have really enjoyed working with him. Everyone at Chelsea knows he was the main reason why I came to England. If Glenn Hoddle had not been in charge as manager I might not be wearing a blue shirt now. For personal reasons I would prefer Glenn to stay at Chelsea. I have really prospered again this season. It has been a marvellous year, one of the best and most joyful in my career. But there is still a lot of work to be done at Chelsea. We have a nice squad, but we need three top European players. Chelsea must act now and buy quickly. I have told the club several times which European players want to play for Chelsea. I have a lot of contacts and I know a lot of the top players in the game. Some of the biggest names in football have rang me and actually begged me to pass their name on.'

Hoddle eventually called his players together and informed them that he had been offered the job as England coach. Two days later he took it. Ruud said: 'It all happened so fast for Glenn and he was given only 48 hours to make up his mind. We discussed it and I told him it was an extraordinary opportunity that rarely comes along. As soon as I heard Hoddle had been offered the job, I knew he would take it. I told him not to concern himself with me or anyone else. He had to do this for himself. It is important that he is an independent person. I'm sure he will handle himself well in the job. At least he has enough money not to worry about things going wrong.'

Hoddle returned for the final days training before the last match of the season against Blackburn. The speculation now intensified that Ruud would be offered the role of player-manager. It was clear that Ruud was interested. And, Gullit was the overwhelming choice of Chelsea's fans. He said: 'I am very honoured by the reaction of the fans and the players, and if the job is offered to me I would have to consider it. Because of all the rumours, it's only natural to think about it and how you would do it. I want to carry on playing but it's not easy to concentrate on your football if you are a manager as well.'

At the time, Gullit promised that he would not join up with Hoddle in the England set-up and would definitely be staying at Stamford Bridge in one capacity or another. 'I can say with 100 per cent certainty that I will stay with Chelsea next season,' he said. 'If there is a new manager or coach here I will be happy to play for him. People appreciate what I am doing and I want to give something back.'

Gullit added: 'The feeling among the players is that we want to continue the style we are playing. We hope that whatever the decision about a new manager will be, we can carry on like that. We don't want to play kick and rush football, so it would be wise for the board to consider someone who has the same ideas that Glenn has.'

In his *Sunday Express* column, Ruud reiterated his future would be with Chelsea: 'Hoddle's departure will have no bearing on my commitment to Chelsea. I made no secret of the fact that his presence was a big factor in me moving to Stamford Bridge, but the fact that he has left will not change anything. It's just one of those things that happens in life. I have a year of my contract to run and will honour it. There are no loopholes or clauses in the deal – I don't want them. I'm enjoying myself greatly with Chelsea. There have been a few jokes about our future. The players have said we don't want so-and-so coming in because we'll have to start running all over the place and a couple of them have started calling me 'gaffer'. It's just a bit of a laugh.'

There were plenty of laughs for Ruud at the Planet Hollywood awards night at the end of the season when devoted Chelsea fan Damon Albarn, of the pop group Blur, presented him with the Best Foreign Player of the Year prize. Damon insisted that Ruud confirm that he would accept the job of player-manager before he handed over the award!

Alan Hansen was in no doubt about Gullit's contribution in his first season. In his *Daily Express* column, he wrote: 'The best newcomer to the Premiership has undoubtedly been Ruud Gullit. I think he has been sensational for Chelsea. His enthusiasm for the game at the age of 33 speaks volumes, and he is still really fit, with sometimes unbelievable pace. His passing, like Cantona's, is on another dimension to what we normally see in this country. He caresses the ball, as Glenn Hoddle used to, and whether it's short or long, the ball is always to a team-mate. Another hallmark of the great player is the way Gullit creates time and space for himself. He can find just that single yard you need when the game is tight and, vitally, can play on either foot. I didn't think we saw the best of him early in the season when he was being used as a sweeper. But when he has played further forward he has impressed me every time I've watched him, always contributing to the collective effort. That's a real star.'

Eventually, Ruud made up his mind that he would take on the extra responsibility. On Friday 10th May, after two hours of talks with Colin Hutchinson, the appointment was confirmed. The following morning, the FA Cup Final between Manchester United and Liverpool was knocked off the back pages of the London editions. The club made the official announcement at 9 pm on Friday, and it was 'hold the back page' in most newspaper offices that night. Bates said: 'I have never seen anything to steal the thunder of the FA Cup Final like this!'

Ruud agreed to sign a new long-term contract and instantly became the highest paid manager in British football without even accepting a penny extra to take the job! Gullit wasn't interested in re-negotiating his terms to take charge of the team. He extended his current two-year contract by a further year and made a verbal commitment to stay long term at Stamford Bridge.

Hutchinson said: 'When I talked to him I jokingly said that he will use his management experience at Chelsea to one day become manager of AC Milan. But he surprised me when he said: 'I don't think so, I hope to stay here for many years to come'.'

Coach Graham Rix was upgraded to work alongside Ruud with the first team, with Gwyn Williams taking the administrative strain as part of the back-up staff. Ruud's priority was to surround himself with people that would enable him to carry on as a Chelsea player; aiming to continue the outstanding form of his first season in the Premiership which made him runner-up to Eric Cantona as Footballer of the Year.

Gullit is in sole control of selecting the team and nominating his transfer targets, while Hutchinson and chairman Ken Bates look after the financial aspects. A key development is the role of Hutchinson. He takes charge of financial matters and the signing of new players. That role did appear to have been allocated to Matthew Harding but, with his well-publicised feud with Bates unresolved, Hutchinson's role has been pivotal in convincing Gullit that the club will run smoothly. Hutchinson was already involved in discussions with Gianluca Vialli, the Juventus captain, who was tempted by a move to London. Gullit's appointment as player-manager might eventually swing a deal in Chelsea's favour.

Bates said: 'It was fairly clear what was going to happen. Ruud went away to think about it, and had a meeting with Colin Hutchinson. They did the deal and within 10 minutes Ruud was on his mobile phone to people in Europe about players he wants to bring in.'

Hutchinson revealed how the club sounded out Gullit, a day before Hoddle officially announced his decision to move to the FA. 'I had a brief chat with Ruud and then had another half-hour with him after the tremendous reception he received after the last match of the season. We went through things with him and then

I gave him six days to sort it all out. When I knew Glenn was leaving, Ruud was one of the people we immediately thought of and it was a unanimous decision by the board to offer the job to him. We were concerned that his playing form didn't drop when he takes charge, so we have named Gwyn Williams to help with things like administration at the training ground.'

The club clearly listened to the wishes of their supporters and acted on them by appointing Ruud. The one thing that Bates and Harding could agree on was that they didn't want George Graham and they did want Gullit!

Chelsea Independent Supporters' Association vice-chairman Mark Pulver felt board-room rows would linger on but said: 'Now the supporters are just hoping that the Gullit factor overrides all the behind-the-scenes problems. Having him at the club will open the door for other stars to come to the club and we are sure that Gianluca Vialli will want to play for him.'

The appointment was particularly well received by the media. The *Daily Mail* supplemented their coverage on Cup Final morning with a article from their chief soccer writer Neil Harmen:

'It was only natural that, once Glenn Hoddle had left to steer his country's course towards the next century, Chelsea would turn to Ruud Gullit to keep Stamford Bridge's body and soul together. If Hoddle was the man who sent the wind of change through the old glamour club and raised his profile to new heights, then his talisman on the field was the dreadlocked Dutchman who was the personification of class and charm ... Gullit has been everything – on the field and off it – that Chelsea could have wanted.

'A superb athlete, who at 33, has shown a remarkable ability to make the Premiership play at his pace, Gullit has the charisma which comes with learning football at the knee of Holland's greats. When an ever-thirsty media have wanted an opinion on anything to do with football, out has stepped Gullit to speak in whatever language has been required. On the opening day of the season, when he wished the English Press a good season, you could hear grown men sighing. Not used to such a friendly face – and someone who talked as good a game as he played – we swooned. But, there is nothing false about Gullit. He simply speaks as he is, with candour, intelligence, wit and common sense. Chelsea could not, in all sincerity, have looked elsewhere. On their doorstep, under their nose, was the man who can help them fulfil the plans that Hoddle had in place, but which had to be put to one side when England came calling ... From their darkness, Chelsea have seen the light.'

The Dutchman's appointment was welcomed by delighted Stamford Bridge players. Scottish international John Spencer said: 'A player of Ruud's standing will influence the club's ability to bring in top-class players. We are already being linked with the likes of Gianluca Vialli. We may have lost a world-class manager in Glenn Hoddle – but we've got another in his place!'

Defender Scott Minto said: 'Ruud's pulling power is even better than Glenn's – he is one of the greatest names in world football. He has been a great success here and I'm sure other foreign players will look at him and want to give it a go themselves. A few years ago the idea of leading world-class players coming to Chelsea was laughable, but not now. The reception he got from the fans in our last game of the season was so great that the other 10 of us ought not to have bothered to go on the pitch.'

Spencer revealed that Gullit's appointment would secure his immediate future at the club, following speculation that he might be on his way back to Scotland. The striker said: 'I have two years left at Chelsea and I'm looking forward to pre-season already so that I can work with Ruud. You cannot fail to learn just by training with him.'

Eddie Newton confirmed that the entire Chelsea team breathed a sigh of relief when the decision was announced. Newton, who missed the latter part of last season through injury, said: 'The players are delighted that Ruud has got the job, but at the same time we're all relieved. He was the only choice, if the good work Glenn had done at Stamford Bridge was to continue. Chelsea have gone through a major transformation under Glenn. If someone else had taken over, it could have spelt disaster.'

But Newton warned his new boss that there can be no more 'Mister Nice Guy' at the Bridge. 'It will be interesting to see how Ruud's relationship with the players changes. He enjoys a good laugh with the lads, and has become something of a practical joker at the club. But he can't afford to have a relationship like that with the players any more.'

Gullit spent the weekend in Amsterdam finalising his new contract with his solicitor, returning in time for the launch of the BBC's summer sporting events; with the new Chelsea boss signed up for his expert analysis for Euro '96. Ruud lined-up with a host of star commentators, including Gary Lineker, at the Roof Gardens Hotel, only to be confronted with the media pack asking searching questions about the renewed feud between Bates and Harding – what a welcome to management on his first official day in office!

Bates, who had ripped up his deal with Harding, said: 'The goalposts kept moving and it was time to put up or shut up. It was better that the uncertainty was resolved. But life has to go on. You can't keep hanging around for the train if it's not going to leave the station. You have to get another train.'

Ruud was as nifty on his feet in dealing with the high profile row as he was quick on his feet eluding Premiership defenders. He demonstrated managerial diplomacy when he did his utmost to ignore the internal squabbling. 'I don't know what they are fighting about and I don't want to know – I don't care. I know Glenn was always concerned about it, and the sooner it's resolved the better for everyone at Chelsea. Although it's nothing to do with the team or the players, it's better to clear it up so everyone can get on with their jobs. Bates and Harding are two proud men and neither is prepared to give in. Things were not resolved and now they have done this. It's not my business. I must be concerned more about the team. I don't know how it will work out, but it must be for the benefit of Chelsea and nothing else.'

He believed that the dispute would not affect his ability to recruit the players he had already made contact with, having notified the club of his list of transfer targets. He said: 'If I get what I need to build a team, I'll be happy – and I've been told there's money available. I've been given all the answers I need – now I hope the club keep their word. Of course I had a lot of questions to ask before I accepted the job. I had to think about it before I said yes, but fortunately I had time to think it over because I had read in the papers that the post might be offered to me. Obviously I will have to work within a budget, but that's my concern. The most important point is that I know how much I can spend to make Chelsea a better team and an even bigger club.

'We have a lot of possibilities of who to buy but you must be careful as a lot of other managers are also looking to sign them. You need a certain kind of player and you hope you can find them in England. But if they are not available, or are too expensive, then you must look somewhere else. I know I will attract good players to Chelsea. Not necessarily star players, but ones who fit in with my ideas and the team.'

Gullit was prepared to smash the Stamford Bridge pay structure in order to land his top transfer targets. He said: 'I'm not interested in how much money a player earns – I'm interested in whether he can do a job for Chelsea. I wouldn't discount someone even if it means paying them more than me. And I don't care whether they are English or European – they could come from Timbuktu for all I care – as long as they fit into our style of play.'

It didn't take long before the procession of star names were walking through the doors at the Bridge…Gianluca Vialli, Frank Leboeuf and Roberto di Matteo.

Ruud explained precisely the way he intends to operate in his new role, and it will be closer to the Continental model than anything ever attempted in English football previously. 'I don't want to be distracted. I'm very excited about this job but I can't afford to underestimate the demands. It's not as if I'll be training every day then going home to rest. For the first time in my career I shall have to adapt to the combined roles and that will take time. I must learn to divide my energy and I'll be curious to see for myself how things go because playing football is still my main role and I don't want my performances on the pitch to suffer. The important thing for me is to make sure I can still perform on the pitch. Nothing must take me away from that. So we will all have to adapt slowly. To this new structure and to ourselves.

'I didn't want to manage the whole club as that is too difficult. You have to be on the phone, do a lot of paperwork and be in the office – and then Chelsea still want me as a player! To do all those jobs would have been impossible, the demands would have been too great. It's certainly a different challenge, and I hope it won't affect how I play. I hope I can handle it and things go well, but you must have the right staff around you. I intend to use the same system as Glenn, with some new players.'

As Ruud embarked on the latest stage of his glittering career, it is clear he has set himself further goals to achieve. He wants to bring success back to Stamford Bridge. Although he has only been in England for a year he has a great affinity with this country's football and its supporters. 'I was very proud to be offered the job at Chelsea because I had been touched by the fans' backing at our last game of the season against Blackburn. Fans have never kissed my boots or knelt down at my feet in homage before like that and it was a very emotional moment, knowing they were all behind me. Glenn told me he had recommended to the board that they give his job to me. With that kind of backing, they made it very easy for me to say, yes.'

CHAPTER THIRTEEN

Message from the Fans and Players

Chelsea is synonymous with celebrity fans. And, they have plenty to say about Ruud Gullit, his influence on Chelsea, and indeed the whole of English football. Gullit even stimulated the usually grey-toned Prime Minister to break out into glorious technicolour enthusiasm. True Blue fan John Major might have his problems with the Scott Report, the All-Party talks to bring a lasting peace in Northern Ireland, and a General Election on the horizon, but he still found time in his hectic schedule to assess the impact of Ruud Gullit on English football and Chelsea in particular.

The Prime Minister issued this message from No 10: 'Ruud Gullit has graced the British game with distinction and his customary elegance this season. We all knew what a good player he was before he came to England but this season we have been fortunate to have observed his skills week in and week out at first hand. The English game and, it goes without saying, Chelsea Football Club, have been lucky to have him here.'

Well, of course, the PM was just slightly biased. He is a Chelsea fan after all. Yet, John Major was reflecting the mood of the football-mad nation that had fallen in love with Ruud's style. The PM was convinced that Gullit had brought a new era at Chelsea. The signing of the one-time World's No1 player, plus the acquisition of other international superstars had the PM purring as Chelsea showed their commitment with hard cash. Even before the 1995/96 season kicked off, John Major was optimistic that Gullit could inspire an end to a quarter of a century without a major trophy for Chelsea. He remarked: 'Chelsea Football Club is not just one of the big clubs in London, it is one of the biggest in Britain. That is why I am very excited by the transfers of Ruud Gullit and Mark Hughes and it is not before time that Chelsea should be regarded among the elite clubs in this country. It is ludicrous to think that Chelsea have won just one Championship – way back in 1955 – and one FA Cup, as long ago as 1970.'

John Major's Dream Team from watching Chelsea for forty years is: Bonetti; P. Sillett, McCreadie, R. Harris, Elliott, Gullit, Hoddle, Greaves, Osgood, Wilkins, Wise.

The House of Commons is full of Chelsea fans. Seb Coe MP, 'ran' through his views on how Gullit has given fresh hope for long suffering supporters. 'An uncle of mine always said that class tells, and this guy has class in abundance. There is no question that he has the ability. I've been to Italy when I've been in training and I had taken the chance to watch Gullit live and he possesses that quality that all the greats have ... they make it look very easy.' Seb had his doubts from the very start that the sweeper position would be permanent. Astutely he said: 'There was no reason on the planet that he couldn't make that position his own, but its vastly different in English football than on the Continent because of the speed of Premier League football. He has vast experience of how the sweeper system operates on the Continent, but there they get far more protection and much more time to dwell on the ball without the Vinny Jones' of this world taking him home as a prize trophy. Yes, of course, he is a big bugger and he has the gifts to dominate the space and not be knocked off the ball.

'It slightly worries me, and this is not trying to down grade the other players, but I remember watching Jimmy Johnstone at Bramall Lane for a couple of seasons and he was putting the ball into areas that he assumed the other players would be, and they were not there. It helps having an experienced player like Mark Hughes up front. I don't expect him to score a hat full of goals all on his own, but he will take the pressure off Spencer, and he will get more goals as a result.'

Seb feels that Gullit is the focal point of the side, just as Hoddle wanted to be. 'When Glenn was out there he made such a difference to the side. He came on for a short time in the Cup Final, and I'm convinced that had he come on much earlier he would have made a big difference. It is a testimony to Glenn that players of real class like Gullit and Hughes were attracted to Chelsea. Such players avoid managers who are not capable of appreciating their special skills, and no-one can accuse Glenn of that!

'You know, genuine Chelsea fans have a great empathy with West Ham supporters. Year after year the chances of winning something important are very slim. Apart from a good cup run now and again you don't expect to see a championship side. But we do expect to see good football. Glenn Hoddle has tapped into the fans psyche more than any other manager in recent times. Over the years, at Chelsea, if we cannot win the top prizes then at least we can console ourselves with having some of the best talent around in English football gracing us at the Bridge. But lets be honest about it, that through much of the 1980s it was pretty average. Now, once again, we expect a Chelsea side to entertain us with good football.'

David Mellor is perhaps the best known of the Chelsea contingent in the House – apart from the Prime Minister, of course. The host of *606 Live* is suffering a resurgence of optimism in Chelsea's chances of glory – and he is deeply worried. 'I've got an 11-year-old in the advanced stages of hysteria!' David advises caution, let-down so often in the past. He explained his reasons. 'I am just determined to be a little pessimistic so that I can be truly delighted if things go well. I'd rather tackle it that way than believe that Ruud Gullit will be our saviour only to discover that at his age it is just a little beyond him.'

There is no doubt in Mellor's mind that Gullit's status is still among the worlds elite. 'He is undoubtedly one of the outstanding footballers of the last 20 years. He would come into the top ten or twelve of the all-time greats in most peoples list, if not near the top.'

David has an ever lasting memory of Gullit, dreadlocks flowing, ripping England apart, and looking every inch the great footballer. 'The game that convinced me that Ruud Gullit was outstanding occurred two European Championships ago, when England were spectacularly unsuccessful, as opposed to being merely unsuccessful. In the build-up to the tournament Holland came to Wembley and Gullit stole the show. His lopping stride took him, seemingly effortlessly, upfront when it mattered, and back in defence when it mattered. Holland were in total command in the first half, while England stormed back in the second. At times it looked as though Gullit was playing England by himself.

'Since then, Gullit has got older and has been knocked about a bit. I'm cautious because of his injury problems over the years. Maybe Hughes will prove to be a better medium term bet than Gullit. Then again Glenn Hoddle himself endured a career ending injury only to come back with a remarkable recovery. He returned from Monaco and worked out at Chelsea before going to Swindon and that gave him an affinity with the club. But no-one expected him to play another game. Also Gullit's temperament has been questioned. Remember the way he sulked when he was substituted by his coach against England and seemed in conflict over the team strategy. I just wish Chelsea had bought him a few weeks after that game.

'Gullit is a huge influence. My only worry is whether he still has the steam left in him. He does mentally, judging by what he has said, and done. Sometimes the spirit is willing only for the flesh to be weak. He seems to have a positive mental attitude to the task. Chelsea were not the only choice available to him, and I am sure Glenn Hoddle was influential in making his decision.'

Will Chelsea win a major trophy? 'There is a real problem because there is a yawning gap between the top four or five clubs and the rest, in terms of resources. Chelsea have come close under Hoddle. An hour into the Cup Final it looked as though they might beat Manchester United. They looked too young and too inexperienced to cope. Perhaps now they have that experience with Gullit and Hughes. But they were not that far away. You cannot write them off. But the tragedy of Chelsea is the inconsistencies. Regardless of who is in the team, it seems a Chelsea side is capable of beating the best in the land and losing to the worst. History is littered with such examples. I hope that will change because I passionately want the club the team to win something. Realistically it is going to be very difficult for any club that doesn't have the resources of the big boys like Liverpool, Arsenal, Newcastle, Blackburn and Manchester United.'

Controversial motor-mouth, Tony Banks is another Chelsea fan in the House. He has nothing but admiration for Hoddle's initiative in getting Gullit. 'He might be in the twilight of his career, but as Glenn Hoddle himself demonstrated there is no substitute for class and someone in their 30s can be more than capable of showing people exactly how its done.

'It may be down to Glenn Hoddle's influence that world class players, and I mean world class, are being attracted to Chelsea. Don't forget that Dennis Bergkamp was talking about pictures of

Glenn Hoddle on his wall as a kid, and how much he would have liked to play for Glenn before he committed himself to Arsenal. It is tremendous that a player of Gullit's standing is at Chelsea. It has created a great deal of excitement, I was going to say among the party faithful, but I mean among the fans.

'My dad first took me to Stamford Bridge, I suppose most dads first take their lads. I was lucky enough to start going the season prior to their championship, and I went to every home game when they won the title, it was quite spectacular. Unfortunately we haven't seen anything since as far as the championship is concerned. That is why Chelsea has such an enormous appetite for success. But there is such desire and determination to be successful and there is a lot of optimism around at the moment. Gullit has created a great deal of interest again in the fortunes of the team. Not since the days of Charlie Cooke, Peter Osgood and Alan Hudson have we had a truly world class star.

'Gullit will help the youngsters to emerge, in the way that Matt Busby encouraged the Busby Babes and Ted Drake began the Chelsea revolution way back in the 1960s with players of the calibre of Jimmy Greaves and Peter Brabrook. It seems to be that clubs these days don't rely on their youth development system as much as they should. The number of foreign players who come to this country has to be watched. Of course we want to see players of the calibre of Klinsmann and Gullit but if we persist in bringing over so many others we shall pay the price of ignoring the development of our own youngsters.'

Chelsea's celebrity fans extend to the entertainment industry, actors and musicians. Suggs from Madness is a prime example. When asked what appeals to him most about Gullit, 'Suggsy' says mischievously: 'He plays bass guitar!' But what of his football prowess? 'I've always admired him from afar. Even before Jurgen Klinsmann came over here, I'd have preferred to have had Gullit in my side rather than any other of the foreign stars – and that includes Eric Cantona. Gullit, for me, is the ultimate footballer. He gets forward for corners, has a bullet header, gets back to defend, can tackle … he's the all-round player.

'Alright he might be getting on a bit, but he is still a powerful force. I'd prefer Gullit at the Bridge to anyone really, even Bryan Robson. We have produced world class stars, but no-one compares with someone like Gullit. He's fabulous. I can hardly believe we've got him at the Bridge. I go to all the Chelsea games, and even once had a column in *Bridge News* until Pat Nevin took over!

'My only worry about foreign superstars is that they can come to our football and go through it like a knife through butter – its just too easy for them. They can turn up, play a few brilliant games and walk off with the Footballer of the Year award. It makes me feel that we can win the league with Gullit in the team. Well, I am always optimistic about Chelsea, you have to be. The English game has become reliant on big strong boys rather than skill, but here we have someone who is a big strong boy, but he can also play.'

It was an emotional downer when Chelsea lost the FA Cup Final two years ago, when Suggs turned up at Wembley in a blue and white wig. Will it now be a Gullit wig? 'Yes, I'll be buying myself one, but I won't be paying a tenner! That's what they're selling those second hand wigs from Holland for. I might think about buying a Gullit shirt. The last Chelsea shirt I bought had two stars on either side of a Lion. I'll tell you how old that one was, we had won the FA Cup. I'll always remember the day we beat Sheffield Wednesday in a thrilling cup tie, but the Cup Final was one of the greatest Chelsea memories – even though we lost. I live in Islington and even in that part of London there was blue and white in every window.'

It seems to Derek Fowlds of *Heartbeat* fame that Chelsea were among the honours at the same time as the period of the popular police series. Its been a long, long time waiting patiently to break 24 years of misery. 'Glenn Hoddle has the style that has brought the club some success and now Gullit and Hughes can bring back excitement and optimism. There is a new buzz of anticipation that the long wait is over for a major trophy. When I watched Gullit play for Holland in his prime he was just simply the most exciting player you could ever possibly find. What a ball player. And, its been some time since we've had a ball player anything like him. The nearest I can recall would be Charlie Cooke and Pat Nevin. But Gullit has got everything, speed, power as well as his tricks on the ball, and Hughes is also international class.

'For so long Chelsea have not been a top Premiership side because they have always fallen two or three players short. Why can't they get top quality players? That's always puzzled me. Instead the Liverpool and Manchester Uniteds are packed with internationals virtually in every position. At last we can boast two players worthy of any team. And with these two in our ranks there is every reason to suppose that we shall be successful.

Derek can boast a long association with the Blues. 'I've been a season ticket holder for 26 years but I've had to give it up with my commitments filming up in Yorkshire. But if I cannot get to games, I'm always there in spirit. And, I can rely on my friend Basil Weissand and my youngest son, 27-year-old Jeremy, to keep me informed. I first went to Chelsea 45 years ago when I was 13. It certainly has been a frustrating time since winning the FA Cup in 1971 and the European Cup Winners Cup the year after. We won the Zenith Cup, which was a great day out at Wembley, and it was wonderful beating Manchester City, but this club is big enough to take the major prizes. Instead we nearly went down to the Third Division. The FA Cup Final against Manchester United was something special but I missed out. I went to the semi-final but we were filming *Heartbeat* the weekend of the Cup Final and I couldn't go to Wembley. I even had a Cup Final ticket but I sold it to a mate. To be fair, we were beaten by the better team.'

Derek Fowlds shares a friendship, a love of golf and Chelsea allegiance with fellow actor Clive Mantle of *Casualty* fame. 'How do you pronounce Gullit?' asked Clive. With a deep, throaty 'h'. So, according to Clive, who plays caring consultant Mike Barrett in the BBC hit hospital series, it's the return of the 'H' bombs at the Bridge. He explained: 'We've always had top players beginning with 'h' ... Houseman, Harris, Hollins, Hinton and Hudson. Now we've got Hullit and Hughes ... and Hoddle, of course! But Hoddle's now departed and Ruud is the boss with three exciting new foreign stars from Italy and France.

'It is the most excited I've been about Chelsea since the late 1960s, early 1970s, since the break up of the team that contained Osgood and Cooke. Gullit, or should I say 'Hullit', is a fantastic player. The fact that the club are able to attract someone of his class and quality is unbelievable. He is precisely the sort of player that Chelsea fans have wanted for a long time. In fact I'd go as far as to say he is probably the best player we have had at the club in the past 20 years.

'Glenn Hoddle must be applauded for this. He is a natural magnet for players of class because he is also a class act in his own right. Gullit's class affects the other players around him, they want to perform to their optimum, they are inspired by playing alongside him. The whole atmosphere of the club has been vastly improved.'

Clive is another long standing fan. 'I've supported Chelsea since the early 1960s but my mum wouldn't let me go until I was over ten. My parents were born in Fulham, but moved out during the war to Barnet. I don't go to the games as much as I would like so I have to keep in touch by *Ceefax*. The FA Cup Final against Manchester United should have been won by Chelsea. If the crossbar had been six inches lower and the referee wasn't from Manchester ... forget about the four goals they scored! Realistically we didn't stand a chance, although we put up a good fight despite the final scoreline.

'Now, at last, with 'Hullit' and Hughes it will be different. 'Hullit' might not be a young man any more, but he can still burst through two or three times during a game. The youngsters at the Bridge can watch him on the training pitch, and surely they will improve their own technique.'

It's still very much a fantasy for David Baddiel to see Chelsea lift one of the major prizes. Ruud has given him fresh hope of a footballing fantasy becoming reality. 'You always want to worship footballers, you feel like that from a little boy, and you never really change. Ruud Gullit is a player I can worship. And, I've not been able to worship a player at Chelsea, I suppose since Alan Hudson.

'Ruud's really cool. I like that. He's really bright. I like that, too. I watched him on his Premiership debut against Everton and I did something unprecedented in my life ... I left the game a few minutes before the end to go straight to the ticket office to make sure I got myself a ticket for the next match at Forest. I don't normally go to many away games, but I wanted to see this guy again. That's how he affected me.

'I have a vague memory of watching Gullit on TV and thought of him as a glorified Bryan Robson, inspirational and powerful, but not mystical in the sense of a Maradona, Cruyff or Pele. Now I've seen him, I was amazed by his exceptional touch, his accurate long-range passes, and his ability to go past players. Certainly he was exceptional when he played in Italy. But I will need to watch him a lot more before I came to any conclusion about his world ranking. For me Maradona, Pele, Cruyff were the tops and I'd even go for Matt Le Tissier!'

David was instantly swept along on Gullit-mania. 'I had not felt like that since the days of Charlie Cooke and Alan Hudson. The nearest I can think who comes close to Ruud is Alan Hudson. There was a player in the same sort of mould, particularly his passing ability. While Peter Osgood might fall into this category, he was more of a target man, albeit a very good target man. But I was really impressed with Gullit's dribbling skills.'

Pride of place for Chelsea fans will be the views of some of the stars of the 1970s, when the Kings Road was last buzzing with a vibrant and exciting team. Hudson was the one of the favourites at the Bridge, now he pens a column for the *Sporting Life*. He described Gullit's signing as 'a masterstroke' as he explained: 'Chelsea have not had a world-class player since Hoddle himself joined them and now Ruud Gullit is the new Messiah at the Bridge. His ability to hit 60 yard passes from one box to the other, with the precision only equalled by Hoddle, is the reason he is such a huge success.'

Hudson knew Gullit would be a smash hit from the very start. 'I watched Gullit in a friendly at Birmingham before the season began and I got goose pimples. I can't really remember the last player who really excited me; Paul Gascoigne to a point, but he's not in this man's class. I was getting pretty disillusioned with football, hearing average players described on TV as great players. But Ruud is one truly great player. At Birmingham, he hit one ball out of defence that never went above six foot in the air. No-one could head it because it was going too quick and it landed in the other box, right at the feet of Mark Stein. I've never seen a player like Gullit; Hoddle was probably the nearest at hitting passes like that, but this fellow goes further.

'He plays where I used to play. It's very hard for people to pick him up. Someone like him only needs that yard of space and he'll murder you. Watch him and see how he gets 10–15 yards of room.'

Hudson is the celebrity host of the club's Drake's restaurant. After the opening game with Everton he told his audience: 'Today you have just seen one of the truly world-class players. He's bringing football back to this country, and it's something we need.'

Peter Osgood was another hero from that last Chelsea side to win a major trophy. For 'Ossie', Gullit offers a glimpse of what Chelsea might be like in the future. Osgood said: 'Boy, what I would give to have played in the same team as Gullit. He has such ability, passing skills and pace. He gets the ball, goes forward then accelerates again. He's exciting and, unusually for so big a star, has time for so many people. It's one outstanding reason for the feeling that Blues have been re-born. But the club badly needs to win something to take off.'

Chelsea's Executive restaurant is named after another old favourite, Roy Bentley. He was guest of honour for the opening match of last season. In the club's official newspaper *Onside*, he said: 'I was so impressed with Gullit. He makes players do things. He gets the ball and sometimes I felt the other players didn't know what he was going to do. But there are times when other players have to make him do things. He had trouble in his own 18 yard box a few times and there was no help. He was okay, he didn't lose it, he twisted and turned. But it's the kind of thing which sends a manager to cigarettes.

'There was a time in the second-half when he was on his own running back deep, and he got caught one against one with Duncan Ferguson. The ball had been lobbed through the middle when the other two defenders had been caught up in attack. He couldn't play it to anybody. He just pulled the thing down, sold a dummy and played it away. Christ, this fella has got something.'

For the opening few months of the season both team-mates and opponents were in awe of the mere presence of Gullit. After a while, he was accepted as one of the lads. He never forced his views about his glorious past and achievements on his new team-mates, but it wasn't long before the players wanted to know about them. To their delight they found Gullit enormously approachable. He enjoys being a teacher, a coach, and will become a top class manager. Dennis Wise observed: 'He's a great fellow, a lovely man. When he first came all the lads were in awe of him, we thought he would do everything, all we had to do was give him the ball. But it wasn't long before he was one of the lads, he doesn't walk around thinking he is above us.'

His special brand of skills and his soccer philosophy made an instant impression at the club. Michael Duberry was the young discovery of the season. He observed: 'Oh yeah, he's definitely one of the boys and I suppose that's quite surprising really. I thought he would just come in and look down his nose at us all, but he's the opposite. He's so down to earth and like the rest of the lads here, he likes a good laugh.' In training there was a friendly yet deadly rivalry between Gullit and Hoddle. Duberry said: 'In the five-a-side games they both wanted to beat each other. But normally we're treated to a load of playground tricks in training. It's not nasty or anything like that. When you've got skill like they have, you don't need to impress anyone.'

Ruud enjoys his role as father figure to the team. The players love it too. He said: 'I bring a lot of experience from my time in Milan. It's nice, when once in a while, the players ask me how it really was at Milan. I explain precisely what we did in training, how hard we really worked. It was truly amazing there, because we had a good team and we played good football, but behind that good football was real hard work, every day. I explained to the players at Chelsea that even though it was such a good team in Milan they did extra work after training. They take really good care of their bodies, they eat well and do all these things to get the right approach.

'The best example I can give is John Spencer. He only seemed to play three games and was always injured. I let him understand that if you are in good shape, you don't have to work so hard during a game, that one or two touches on the ball is better than four or five, trying to dribble and get injured. He's not doing that any more. As I told him, let the ball do the work, because the ball never gets tired and that it's best sometimes to play with your brain. Now he is in the right place at the right time.'

Spencer appreciates the guidance from Gullit. In fact he considers himself fortunate to have received an education in football 'that money just can't buy'. Long after the rest of the players are heading home after training, Gullit spent countless hours working on the pint-sized striker's skills, passing on the kind of tips which made Marco van Basten a world-beater. Spencer says: 'Ruud has been brilliant with me. Since he arrived we've got on well and after training we work on skills for an hour or so. He'll show me all the things he learned in the *Serie A*, wee things which make such a big difference at the highest level. He'll stand 10 yards away with a ball and tell me to skip from side to side. Then he'll throw it and I have to jump up and control it with my instep. It sounds obvious but Ruud says Marco van Basten was a master at that one and scored countless goals with it. The difference is I would usually have taken a ball like that on my chest, then waited for it to come down before I had it under control. Doing it Ruud's way gives you the extra split second which can mean getting a shot away before you're tackled. He's also taught me how to jump and bring the ball down on my chest so that when I land the ball is there as well. Sometimes one of his tricks will come off for me in a game and I think to myself that the big man was right. It's a brilliant education for me. It may only improve my game by a few per cent but I don't care. Money couldn't buy me a tutor like Ruud.'

Gullit's relationship with his Chelsea team-mates developed throughout the season. He says: 'I talk to them a lot. I always say: 'If I criticise you that means I like you, because if I think you have possibilities as a player then I want to help you'. I think your best friend is a friend who can be negative, who can say I don't want you to do that.'

David Lee has grown in stature with the help of Gullit. 'People like Ruud and Sparky (Mark Hughes) have always got time for you. If you do something wrong in the game they won't shout and scream, they'll just quietly point things out. Ruud, for instance, has taken Dubes (Michael Duberry) under his wing and helped him a lot.'

Duberry nods his shaven head in agreement. 'I've picked up several things from him – except his hairstyle.'

Gavin Peacock provides an insight into the relationship between Gullit and Hoddle. He observed: 'Glenn has said in the past that it was like a meeting of minds when they first met. Ruud is a very strong personality and he's always going to have firm opinions but there was no way he was the coach on the pitch and Glenn was the coach off it. Ruud is our leader on the pitch, as was Glenn when he was playing.' Hoddle encouraged input from all his players, even during half-time.

'Glenn let us have our say before he comes into the dressing-room,' said Eddie Newton. 'Then he'd come in and say: 'Right, I've heard a few things being said while I was outside. Some are good and some are bad but this is what I think'. When that happened, Ruud listened along with everybody else. When Ruud does speak everyone respects what he has to say.'

Nigel Spackman says: 'Glenn did things his own way but he

maybe chatted to Ruud on a one-to-one basis. Ruud has won every accolade in the game but in football it doesn't matter how old you are, you never stop learning.'

Striker Mark Stein has marvelled at the Dutch maestro's ability. Stein said: 'I had seen Ruud play many times on television, but it's not until you are actually alongside him that you really begin to appreciate his genius. His passing ability is incredible. He can drop you an inch perfect ball from all of 50 yards. The weight of his passing is quite unbelievable, I think he has built-in radar! He has already been an inspiration to everyone in the team. The gaffer wanted us to play a certain style last season, but perhaps no-one really had the confidence to do it. Now we have seen how Ruud plays, and it is giving others the confidence to try the same thing. There is an aura about the guy.'

Gavin Peacock explained Gullit's influence within the Chelsea camp. 'He is such a big personality. He speaks his mind, and is on the same wavelength as the rest of the players. He is always approachable. Because he is so fluent in languages, he can give and take all the banter. It really is a privilege to be around him.' Exactly how does he influence a team? 'Players are always asking about his days at Milan,' Peacock said. 'And he will tell you how they did it there. He talks about diet and fitness and, as well as listening, you find yourself watching him in training to see how he makes space, which is one of the strong points of his game. You also pick up points about stretching and flexibility. Sometimes at the beginning of training, Peter Shreeves will say 'right, let's see how Ruud warms up' and we'll take it in. A lot of what he has he is naturally blessed with. Which isn't to say he doesn't work hard. But it's like the gaffer, you can't quite put your finger on some of it. Ruud is very strong and quick, a magnificent athlete.

'It was a fascinating enough experience for the Chelsea players with Gullit in the dressing room as "one of the lads". It threatens to be even more enlightening with Gullit in charge, able to put into practice his own philosophies of how the game should be played – and with his own formidable recruits Vialli, Lebouef and Di Matteo.'

Career Highlights

1962	Born 1 September 1962 to father George Gullit and mother Ria Dil. At birth he is registered and named Rudi Dil. He later changes his name to Ruud Gullit.
1969	Joins junior club Meerboys. Then moves on to DWS Amsterdam.
1979	Signs for the professional club Haarlem. Makes his league debut at the age of 16. The club is relegated to the Dutch Second Division in his first season.
1980/81	Haarlem win promotion back to the First Division. Gullit scores 14 goals and is voted the Second Division's Player of the Year.
1981/82	Haarlem finish 4th in Division One. Makes his international debut, on his 19th birthday, in a 2–1 defeat against Switzerland in Zurich. In April 1982 signs for Feyenoord for £300,000.
1982/83	He scores his first goal for Holland in a 2–1 victory against The Republic of Ireland.
1983/84	Feyenoord sign Johan Cruyff and he inspires the team to the League and Cup double. Gullit plays in his first European competition – the UEFA Cup for Feyenoord.
1985/86	Gullit moves to PSV Eindhoven who win the League championship. Ruud plays as sweeper that season and scores 24 goals.
1986/87	PSV again win the League title but Gullit is unhappy at the club and asks for a transfer. He is sold to AC Milan for a world record fee of £5.5 million
1987/88	AC Milan win their first League championship in a decade. At the end of the season Gullit inspires the Dutch national side to victory in the European Championships. In the final Gullit scores one of the goals in the 2–0 victory over the USSR. He is voted World and European Footballer of the Year.
1988/89	AC Milan win the European Cup, beating Steaua Bucharest 4–0 in the final – Gullit scoring twice. He had injured his knee in the semi-final victory over Real Madrid and required key-hole surgery to

enable him to be fit for the final.

1989/90 Further operations on his troublesome knee mean long lay-offs and doubts about his career. Yet he recovers in time to win a second successive European Cup winners' medal. AC Milan also win World Club Championship and the European Super Cup. At the end of the season Holland are one of the favourites for the World Cup in Italy but they are knocked out by West Germany in a controversial match.

1990/91 Gullit successfully returns from injury and plays 31 games, but scores only 2 goals. For the first time since Gullit joined the club, Milan fail to win a domestic or European trophy. They do, however, regain the World Club Championship.

1991/92 AC Milan regain the League title. However, Holland fail to regain the European Championship and are beaten in the semi-finals by the eventual winners, Denmark.

1992/93 AC Milan win the championship for the second successive year and reach the final of the European Cup. However, Gullit is left out of the side to face Marseille in the final. Milan lose 1–0.

1993/94 Gullit moves to Sampdoria yet such was his stunning return to form that AC Milan re-sign him. Before the start of the World Cup in the USA, Gullit walks out of the Dutch training camp and retires from international football.

1994/95 He re-joins Sampdoria and he leads them to victory in the Italian Cup final.

1995/96 Available on a free transfer Gullit moves to the Premiership and signs for Chelsea. He finishes runner-up to Eric Cantona for Player of the Year. Chelsea reach the semi-final of the FA Cup to be beaten by Manchester United. At the end of the season manager Glenn Hoddle leaves the club to become England coach. Gullit takes over as Chelsea boss.

Summary (up to end of 1995/96 season)		
	Apps	Goals
Haarlem	91	32
Feyenoord	85	30
PSV Eindhoven	68	46
AC Milan	151	48
Sampdoria	53	24
Chelsea	40	6
TOTALS	488	186
Holland 65 caps 16 goals		

Index